W9-BRH-553

A Short Course

on

Computer Viruses

by Dr. Frederick B. Cohen

Contents

1

0.1   Introduction

This book was derived from recordings of my one-day short courses
on computer viruses. The course runs about 8 hours, and at the
time of this writing, had been taught about 50 times. In this course,
I try to avoid the deep technical details and most of the mathematics behind the conclusions presented. At the same time, I think it
is important to provide enough evidence to be convincing and un-
derstandable. As an aid to the technically inclined reader, I have
provided a number of good references which contain more detailed
technical information.

This is not a technology book, it is a science book. By that I
mean that the purpose of the book is to educate the reader, so that
for the rest of their life, they will understand about computer viruses,
and never be surprised by what happens. For that reason, I avoid
discussing details of particular technologies except for the purpose
of providing examples. The point is to give you knowledge of the
subject that can be applied regardless of the system you are using,
the programming languages in the environment, or the most popular
operating system of the day.

The intended audience is anyone who works intimately with computers on a day-to-day basis. It will be particularly helpful to computer programmers, information systems managers, systems administrators, EDP auditors, and computer security specialists, but it
would also be a good book for an undergraduate student who has
taken a course on computers.

You will find the coverage of this book quite broad. We begin
with the basics of computer viruses, and discuss how they work,
what they can do, and how they are different from other technologies. We then discuss scientific experiments with viruses, viruses
that have appeared in the real world, and how organizations have
historically responded to the threat of viruses. Next, we go into de-

tails about defenses, starting with theoretically sound defenses, then moving into a series of examples of defenses that don't work very well, describing the best current defenses in real systems, and discussing non-technical defenses and management issues. Next we discuss the impact of computer viruses on exposure analysis, go through a series of scenarios that consider viruses in a variety of real-world situations, and sum up the course. Finally, in the appendices, we tell 'the good joke' that I tell just after lunch to wake people up before starting the second half of the course, and provide a list of about 75 annotated references to related works.

I hope that you enjoy this book, and I welcome your comments and suggestions. For those of you interested in getting the software provided with the short course, it can be purchased directly from ASP press, either with the book or separately.

Chapter 1

Computer Virus Basics

1.1 What is a Computer Virus?

I would like to start with a formal definition ...

$\forall M \forall V (M, V) \in VS \Leftrightarrow [V \in TS] and [M \in TM] and$
$\quad [\forall v \in V[\forall H_M[\forall t \forall j$
$\qquad [1) P_M(t) = j and$
$\qquad 2) \square_M(t) = \square_M(0) and$
$\qquad 3) (\square_M(t, j), ..., \square_M(t, j+ \mid v \mid -1)) = v]$
$\Rightarrow \quad [\quad \exists v' \in V[\exists t' > t[\exists j'$
$\qquad\quad [1)[[(j'+ \mid v' \mid) \le j] or [(j+ \mid v \mid) \le j']] and$
$\qquad\quad 2) (\square_M(t', j'), ..., \square_M(t', j'+ \mid v' \mid -1)) = v' and$
$\qquad\quad 3) [\exists t'' s.t. [t < t'' < t'] \ and$
$\qquad\qquad [P_M(t'') \in j', ..., j'+ \mid v' \mid -1]$
$\quad]]]] \ ] \quad] \ ] \qquad] \quad]$

Figure 1.1: Formal Definition

So much for that! Now let me tell you what it means.

9

$$\forall v \in V, v \Rightarrow v', v' \in V$$

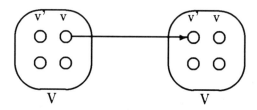

Figure 1.2: Picture of the Formal Definition

When we talk about computer viruses in the deepest sense, we are talking about sequences of symbols in the memory of a machine in whatever form that may be, main memory, the registers, disk, tape, or what have you. What makes one of those sequences of symbols an element of a 'viral set' (V) is that when the machine interprets that sequence of symbols (v), it causes some other element of that viral set (v') to appear somewhere else in the system at a later point in time. Most of the viruses you have probably heard about form singleton viral sets (e.g. sequences of instructions in machine code for the particular machine that make exact copies of themselves somewhere else in the machine), but that's not the only possibility.

- You can have viruses that are not in the binary code of the machine; an example is a viruses written in a source language that infects other source language programs. Any sequence of symbols that is interpreted on the machine could potentially contain a virus.

- All viruses are not from singleton viral sets. You can have viruses that evolve through a finite number of different instances. In fact, you can have viruses that evolve through a potentially infinite number of different versions. It turns out that this is very important, because it makes the problem of virus detection and eradication far more difficult than it would be if we could only make viruses that made exact copies of themselves.

1.2 How does a virus spread through a system?

The working definition of a virus that most people see, goes like this: "A virus is a program that can 'infect' other programs by modifying them to include a, possibly evolved, version of itself".

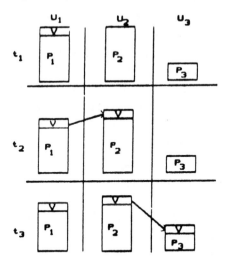

Figure 1.3: A Timesharing System

Let's look at an example. We have here a picture of a timesharing system with three users; U_1, U_2, and U_3; who own three programs; P_1, P_2, and P_3 respectively; at times t_1, t_2, and t_3. If at time t_1 program P_1 is infected with a virus V, and at time t_2 user U_2 runs program P_1, then because user U_2 is authorizing program P_1 to act on U_2's behalf, and user U_2 has the authority to modify program P_2, the virus in program P_1 is authorized to modify program P_2, and thus it infects program P_2. Similarly, if at time t_3 user U_3 runs program P_2, program P_3 becomes infected. Thus the virus spreads from program to program and from user to user.

Note that this operates in a typical timesharing computer environment, even with standard protection mechanisms in place. This means that the protection mechanisms used throughout the computing community today are inadequate for defense against viruses.

To present this to people with a non-technical background, we use the secretaries analogy. In this analogy we talk about a group of secretaries, where each secretary does their job by taking orders from their boss. For example, a boss might tell secretary 3 to "make a call". When secretary 3 gets that order, secretary 3 looks for a notecard that says "make a call" at the top, and does whatever that notecard says. If secretary 3 doesn't have such a notecard, then secretary 3 will ask the other secretaries if they have a "make a call" notecard. When secretary 3 finds such a notecard, he or she does whatever that notecard instructs.

Now let's imagine that somewhere in the middle of one of these notecards was the following sentence:

"In your own words, copy this sentence onto all your other notecards, and if the date is after January 1, 1991, burn everything in sight".

Let's see what happens. When, for example, secretary 2 is told to write a memo, this sentence is going to be interpreted in the process of writing that memo, and all of secretary 2's notecards are going to become infected. If at a later time, secretary 3 is told to make a call,

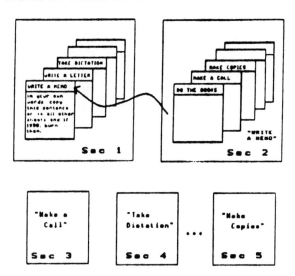

Figure 1.4: The Secretaries Analogy

all of secretary 3's notecards become infected, and so on. So this virus spreads from notecard to notecard, from secretary to secretary, from office to office (as secretaries change jobs), and eventually from multi-national firm to multi-national firm.

On January 2, 1991, there are going to be a lot of fires!

Let's look at it from a programmer's point of view using a "pseudo-code" example of the computer virus. The reason I use pseudo-code examples instead of actual codes from computer viruses is that, in 1983 when we first developed these models, I made the decision that it would be inappropriate to reveal the actual code of an attack. The reason is that an attacker could make a copy, modify it slightly to do damage, and then we might be in big trouble. So, rather than give the attackers the code for an attack, I decided to show the defenders what the attack might look like so they could provide appropriate defenses without giving the attackers an obvious entry. Unfortunately, the response of the computer science community was denial. They felt that such a thing was not possible. As recently as 1989, there was a dominant feeling that this was just "a lot of media hype". In the meanwhile, the attackers read the early papers, and took action to realize many attacks. This situation is changing because of the large number of real-world attacks, and the computer science community is now beginning to think that viruses are a realistic possibility.

```
Program V :=
{1234567;
Subroutine infect-executable:=
 {loop: file=random-executable;
 if (first-line of file = 1234567)
   then goto loop;
   else prepend V to file;}

Subroutine do-damage:=
 {whatever damage you can program}
Subroutine trigger-pulled:=
 {whatever trigger you want here}

Main-program-of-virus:=
 {infect-executable;
 if (trigger-pulled) then do-damage;
 goto next;}
next:
}
```

The pseudo-code virus V works like this. It begins with a marker "1234567" This is not necessary, but in this particular case, it is used to identify that this particular virus has already infected a program, so that it doesn't infect the same program repeatedly. It then has three subroutines followed by the main program. The main program of the virus starts by infecting another program through the subroutine "infect-executable". This subroutine loops, examining random executable files until it finds one without the first line "1234567". When it finds an uninfected executable, *V* copies itself into the beginning of the previously uninfected executable, thus infecting it.

Note that there have been tens of thousands of readers of this particular example, and yet nobody has ever called to attention the fact that it will loop indefinitely once all of the executable files in the system are infected. That is easily changed.

After infection, the virus checks for a "trigger pulled" condition, which can be anything the attacker programs in. If the condition is active, it performs whatever damage is programmed into the 'do-damage' routine. Finally, the main program of the virus jumps into whatever program the virus was 'prepended' to when it was installed, and runs that program normally. So, if this virus is at the beginning of an executable program, and you run that program, the virus is going to attach itself to the beginning of the next program, and if the trigger is not pulled, it's just going to run the program it was attached to the beginning of. If this process happens relatively quickly, users are not likely to notice it taking place during the normal operation of a system.

1.3   What Damage Could A Virus Do?

Let's take a cursory look at the types of damage you might get from
a computer virus.

```
Trigger-pulled:=
 {if the date is after Jan 1, 1991;}

Do-damage:=
 {loop: goto loop;}
```

This is a simple denial of services example. The triggering condition in this case is time driven, and the damage is an infinite loop.
If this virus spread throughout a computer system or network, then
as of the triggering date, every program that was infected would go
into an infinite loop. So, in a typical computer system as systems
exist today, that means every program on your entire network would
stop operating as of that moment.

This is only the simplest and most obvious sort of attack, it is
relatively easily detected and countered, and does not require much
sophistication to write, but as we will now begin to see, the situation
can get somewhat more complex. Here is a more interesting virus
called a "Compression Virus". We use this example, because it shows
us a couple of things about typical ideas for defenses, particularly
that it is not such an easy matter to determine whether a program
has been infected.

```
   Program CV:=
     {01234567;
     subroutine infect-exec:=
        {loop:
         file=random-exec-file;
         if first-line of file = 01234567
            then goto loop;
(1)      compress file;
(2)      prepend CV to file;
        }
     main-program:=
        {if ask-permission
            then infect-exec;
(3)      uncompress rest-of-file;
(4)      run uncompressed file;
        }
     }
```

This virus works in a four step process, marked 1,2,3, and 4 in the code. Rather than look at the code for this attack, I think it is much easier to look at the picture.

We start at a time t_0 with program P_1', the infected version of program P_1, and a clean program P_2 that has never been infected with this virus. If at time t_1, program P_1 is run, the following steps take place.

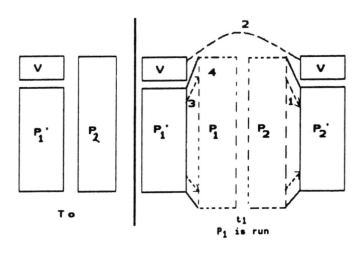

Figure 1.5: A Compression Virus

1. Program P_2 is compressed into P_2' using a standard file compression routine.

2. CV attaches itself to the beginning of P_2'.

3. P_1' is decompressed into the original program P_1.

4. The original program P_1 is executed normally.

There are a couple of things to note about this particular compression virus. One thing is that the size of P_2' is typically about 1/2 the size of the original P_2. That is, file compression typically saves about 50% of the space taken up by files (sometimes you can get 2/3 or more). The net effect is that if you spread this virus throughout a computer system, you can save about half the space taken up by programs. The penalty you pay for that space savings is that whenever you run a program, it has to decompress, and this takes extra time. So the compression virus implements a time/space tradeoff in your computer system, and in this sense might be quite useful.

Now suppose we have a defender that is trying to figure out whether a file is infected, and an attacker who is willing to put forth some effort to prevent this detection. One of the earliest defenses we saw in the real-world, was looking to see if the size of a file changed. A lot of people wrote papers saying "To find viruses, look for changes in the size of the files." Well, let's see what the attacker can do to avoid that. Since the resulting program P_2' has fewer bytes than the original P_2, by simply adding appropriate null bytes to P_2', we can make P_2' exactly the same size as the original program P_2, and therefore, the size of the program has not changed.

Suppose the defender uses a simple checksum to indicate changes in a file. A simple checksum is formed by adding up all the bytes in the file in some modulus. By taking an initial checksum, and then comparing at a later date, defenders try to detect viruses. Well, instead of putting in null bytes (as we did to keep the file size identical), we can put in any other bytes we wish. In particular, we can put in bytes that make the checksum of the infected program the same as the checksum of the original. Then a simple checksum will not detect the presence of a virus. So simple checksumming is very easy to avoid as well.

The same is true for CRC codes. A CRC code is typically used to identify changes on disks from random errors, but of course, it is only useful against random Gaussian types of noise, and will not work against serious attackers because it is very easy to forge a modification that keeps the same CRC code as the original program.

It turns out that it is pretty straightforward to write a virus so that the resulting size, the modification date and time (on most systems), the checksum, and the CRC code for the infected file, are exactly the same as for the original. This points out some of the difficulty in trying to detect the sorts of change that a virus might make to a file.

1.4   Some Other Things Viruses Might Do

Now I just want to go through some other types of damage very quickly, to give you an idea of the range of things you might expect from computer viru s attacks. Of course, when I get to the end, you will probably be thinking of lots of other things that a virus could do. So, have a good time. Just realize that the attackers are also having a good time thinking about these things.

1.4.1   A Data Diddling Virus

Let's start out with the "data diddling" virus. A data diddling virus is a virus where every infected program modifies one bit in one randomly selected data file once a week. In a typical personal computer system there will be something like a thousand infected programs, so each of those thousand infected programs modifies one bit of data from a randomly selected data file once a week. So a thousand randomly selected bits of data in your system are being changed every week.

Is anybody here going to notice that occurring in their system? Does anybody have any system in place to detect the random changing of a bit in a data file? Okay, so if this sort of a virus entered your system, you wouldn't even notice that the damage was being done. You wouldn't notice the virus and you wouldn't notice the damage. Eventually, you would. After a couple of months, or depending on how you use your system, a couple of weeks, you would start to notice that you had all sorts of errors in your database; and you would probably have some difficulty tracking down the source of those errors. In fact, it is very difficult to figure out that these errors come from this virus, because there is no direct link between the attack and the damage, so the symptom does not indicate the cause.

Instead of a random data diddling virus, you could create a far more sophisticated data diddling virus. For example, a virus that randomizes the second and last digits of numbers that look like postal codes, would cause mailing lists to direct mail incorrectly. A virus that switches digits before and after a decimal point, would wreak havoc on most arithmetic calculations. Exchanging commas with periods in a document would cause a condition that would first corrupt information, and subsequently correct it (after changing commas to periods, it would change them back again, alternating between right and wrong versions). This could be quite unnerving.

As an example, a real world virus called "Typo" creates typing errors whenever the user types faster than 60 words per minute.

These data diddling viruses show a key factor in the success of a virus; to make the link between cause and effect so indirect, that it is not likely to be determined by examining results. Thus, even once corruptions are detected, it may be a long time before the cause is determined. The more indirect the link, the more complex the process of tracking down the source. Furthermore, the cost of trying to restore integrity from a data diddling attack might be very high. For example, there is no simple way to determine how far back you have to go to correct those corruptions.

1.4.2 The Random Deletion Virus

The "Random Deletion Virus" is a virus that spreads throughout a system and looks for files that haven't been accessed in, let's say the last month and a half, and deletes them. It turns out that if you haven't accessed a file in the last month and a half, you probably won't access that file in the next month and a half. To the extent that you don't notice that the file is missing, it might be a long time before you determine that it is missing, and you might have great difficulty tracing it to an appropriate backup. In fact, you'll probably think that you deleted it by accident and start to lose confidence in what you have and have not done.

Let's take it a step further. Suppose you have a system in place where in order to save space, you periodically move unaccessed files to off-line backups and then delete them from the system. If the attacker is aware that this system is in place, it's very straight forward to look for files that are about to be moved off line and delete a small percentage of them, say one out of ten. The net effect is that the user gets messages that various files were moved off line, and they figure that everything is nice and safe, it's only off line. When they go to get the file back, they find it's not there! It's not on the system and it's not on the off-line backups and nobody knows where it went, or why it is gone. That could create a few problems, and it almost certainly would not be attributed to a virus without a great deal of effort over a long period of time.

1.4.3   A Production Destruction Virus

A "Production Destruction Virus" is a virus launched, for example, by one steel company against another. In this particular scenario, you launch a virus that spreads through your competitor's company, identifying their production line system and causing the temperature in the third phase of their steel cooling process to be off by ten degrees centigrade on Tuesday afternoons when there are between two and five people using their system, and no system administrator or security administrator logged in.

The net effect is that they'll have lower quality steel and if they go and try and trace down the problem, the chances are, they'll have an administrator on the system looking for the problem and the problem won't occur. It might be very difficult to track down the problem, and in the meanwhile, a noticeable degradation in quality might occur.

1.4.4   A Protection Code Changing Virus

A "Protection Code Changing Virus" is a virus that spreads throughout an environment changing the protection state of the machine; making unreadable things readable; making readable things unreadable; making executable programs readable and writable, and so on.

It turns out that in most modern systems, the protection state of the machine is very complex and there are no adequate tools for determining its propriety or restoring it to a known state. Thus by randomizing the protection state, it is unlikely that the attack will be detected, and it may be very hard to restore the proper protection state. A minor improvement in protection tools would dramatically change this situation, and this is one of the major problems we face today in the information protection area.

1.4.5   A Network Deadlock Virus

A "Network Deadlock Virus" (we've seen this many times in the real world) is a virus that replicates so quickly that it deadlocks a network. All of the network deadlock viruses we are aware of (whether from a bug as in the ARPAnet deadlock of the mid 1970s and the AT+T crash of 1990, or from an intentional attacker as in the IBM Christmas card of 1988 and the Internet virus of 1989) have caused deadlock accidentally.

1.4.6   An Executive Error Virus

One of my favorites is the "Executive Error Virus". This is a virus launched by, let's say the Vice President of R&D, that resides in a cell in a spreadsheet. It's not a virus in the spreadsheet binary executable program, it's in the spreadsheet itself. What it does, is spread from spreadsheet to spreadsheet until it gets to one of the President's spreadsheets. When it gets to one of the President's spreadsheets, it randomly changes one of the cells in the spreadsheet every time somebody looks at it. As a result, the President makes improper decisions based on the wrong numbers in the spreadsheet, and eventually makes so many incorrect decisions that s/he gets fired, and the Vice President moves up!

A similar thing was reportedly done when two partners in a small business attacked a third partner. According to the story, the third partner got so frustrated from errors in programs, that he quit the company. Now this is just a rumor as far as I can tell, but it makes the point.

1.4.7   A Covert Channel Virus

Another interesting virus is a "Covert Channel Virus" used to leak secrets from the best computer security systems available today. Let's talk about these "best computer security systems". Typically, we're talking about a system intended to protect secrecy. It's called a security system, but I will call it a secrecy system. It works like this; if you are at a given secrecy level, you can't read information that's more highly classified, lest it would be leaked to you, and you can't write information that's less highly classified, lest you could leak secrets out to someone else. Here's a picture of such a system.

This is commonly called the "Bell-LaPadula Model" of computer security and it's usually used on systems like RACF, ACF2, Top Secret, and other commercial and military systems.

Now suppose that the least trusted user in this system puts a virus into a program. As soon as a classified user runs that unclassified program, a classified program can become infected. This is because

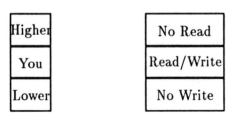

Figure 1.6: A Bell-LaPadula System

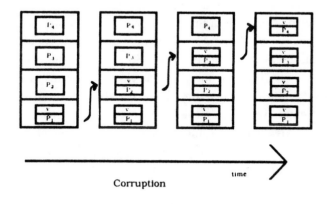

Figure 1.7: A Virus In A Bell LaPadula Based System

there's no rule that says that a more trusted user can't run a less trusted program. The system allows the classified user to run the unclassified program, hence authorizing the unclassified program to act as a classified user and infect the classified program.

Similarly, when a secret user runs the classified program, a secret program can become infected and when a top secret user runs a secret program, top secret programs can become infected. That means that the least trusted user is the most dangerous from the standpoint of a viral attack.

So how do we use that to leak secrets? We do it through something called covert channels. A covert channel is a channel for sending information around a system, that's not normally intended to be an information channel.

Let me give you an example. Suppose a top secret user wants to send information to an unclassified user by using a disk space covert channel. All the top secret user has to do is use a lot of disk space to indicate a '1', and very little disk space to indicate a '0'. If there is an unclassified user on that same computer system, that unclassified user could look at how much disk space is available. If there's very little disk space available, that indicates a '1'. If there's a lot of disk space available, that indicates a '0'. So that's a covert channel.

It turns out that on any system that allows users to share resources in a non-fixed fashion, there are always covert channels. In some systems, simple to exploit channels exist, like top secret file names that are visible to unclassified users. Other signaling mechanisms such as presence of a file or availability of a resource are commonly available even in the most carefully designed systems.

It turns out that in the best computer security systems we have today, covert channels typically allow somewhere around ten bits per second each, and we typically have something like a thousand well-known covert channels in any given system. This means you can leak secrets through covert channels at a combined rate of about ten thousand bits per second, faster than a 9600 baud modem can transmit information. It also turns out that (from Shannon's 1948 paper on information theory) no matter how much noise is in the channel, we can reliably leak secrets, with the bandwidth limited by the signal to noise ratio.

So how do we use these two things to launch an attack? If the least trusted user launches a virus, the virus can spread up through the system until a copy of the virus gets into the top secret area. At that point, this copy of the virus can start transmitting top secret information through the covert channel to a cooperating process in the untrusted environment. So you can leak secrets from the best computer security systems we have, if those systems do not maintain their integrity.

1.5 Viruses in Computing Environments

We're now going to translate the secretaries analogy into the language of a number of modern systems to clarify just how an infection might work, and to convince you that the principle is the same regardless of the particulars of your system.

1.5.1 Viruses in MVS

This is how the virus might work in an MVS system. Suppose that one module somewhere in a private MVS library (e.g. a Fortran subroutine, an object module, a library module, a source program, a spreadsheet that's interpreted by a spreadsheet program, or a database macro) is infected. As the owner (user A) uses the infected module, other modules in A's private library become infected, and as they are used, still other modules become infected, and so on, until eventually, everything in the library that can become infected does become infected. You can easily write a program to do this, it

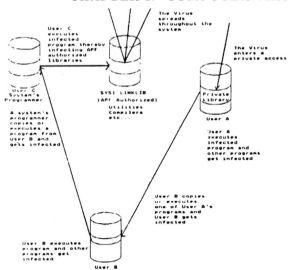

Figure 1.8: An MVS Virus

doesn't violate any security rules, nothing in it will trigger any errors or warnings on the system, and provided the process is reasonably fast, no obvious system changes will be noticed.

Eventually, some other user (user B) might run one of user A's infected programs, use an infected library or spreadsheet macro, or you name it. When user B uses something belonging to user A, then user B's private library may become infected. User B's files start to have copies of the infection and it spreads throughout user B's area, eventually infecting everything that can become infected.

Through this process, the virus can spread from user to user and eventually work its way through the system. However, in some cases, the problem can get much worse very quickly. If some user along the way, say user C, happens to have authority to modify programs or other information in common use, then the virus will spread far more quickly. For example, a system's programmer that runs an infected program, links with an infected library, interprets an infected spreadsheet, uses an infected database, you name it, grants the virus authority to modify system programs. In an MVS system, the virus will eventually spread into one of those system programs and everybody will become infected.

1.5.2 PC, MacIntosh, and Amiga Viruses

In a PC DOS based system, a virus can be planted in an 'EXE' or 'COM' file (binary executables), in a Basic program, a spread sheet, the boot sector, system memory, a device driver, video memory, the on-board clock memory, CMOS memory, or even in unused portions of a disk. Just as in the MVS case, whenever infected information is used, it can infect other information, but in a typical DOS environment, there is no protection, so any reachable information can be infected. If a floppy disk or a network is involved, viruses can spread to these media, and thus move from system to system.

The MacIntosh environment has a very different user interface than DOS, but in terms of operating system protection, it is not very different. It has minimal protection, and that protection is easily bypassed. The MacIntosh environment also has some extra problems related to the fact that some 'data' files have implicit programs which are interpreted each time they are read or written. Viruses in these code segments can be very hard to track down.

The Amiga environment is similar in many ways to the DOS environment, and operating system protection is again minimal and easily bypassed. Thus the Amiga operating system can be corrupted just as the DOS and MacIntosh environments. The Amiga has an extra problem in that every time a disk is put into the system, a program on that disk is read in order to be able to interpret the contents of the disk. Each disk essentially carries its own driver, which means that the Amiga automatically installs and runs programs from the floppy disks whenever they are placed in the machine. Viruses planted in the driver area of a floppy disk are thus automatically installed and run.

1.5.3   Viruses in Unix and VMS

In a Unix or VMS system, a virus can be planted in the same way as in an MVS system, except that instead of modules in a library, viruses typically reside in files in a directory. When an infected file is interpreted, it can infect other accessible files. Viruses can also reside in processes, infecting information accessible by the process. Spreading from user to user can take place whenever a user uses another user's information, just as in MVS. If user A has an infected program, and it is used by user B, then by using user A's program, user B authorizes it to modify user B's programs. Just as there are systems programmers in MVS, there are privileged users in Unix and VMS, and the accelerated spread works in essentially the same manner.

Remember, in each of these examples, the virus doesn't require any special privileges, it doesn't have to modify the operating system, it doesn't depend on any flaw in the operating system implementation, and it doesn't do anything that's not permitted by the security system. The virus spreads because the protection policies in these systems don't protect integrity.

1.6   The Three Differences

There are three major differences between viruses and everything that came before them; generality, extent, and persistence. We will now describe these differences in some detail.

The first major difference is generality. When we look at computer security problems historically, we see things like a flaw in the operating system so that if a user calls a particular system facility in a particular way, then the system will grant access to a part of memory the user is not suppose to access. That's a typical attack before viruses.

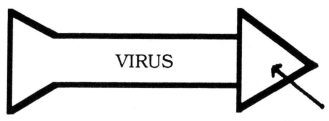

Figure 1.9: A Virus is Like a Missile DAMAGE

With viruses however, we have a very general attack situation. The virus spreads without violating any protection policy, while it carries any desired attack code to the point of attack. You can think of it as a missile, a general purpose delivery system that can have any warhead you want to put on it. So a virus is a very general means for spreading an attack throughout an entire computer system or network.

The second major difference between viruses and previous attacks is their range. We used to think that if somebody broke into Joe's computer account, they could read what Joe could read and write what Joe could write, and that was that. When we did risk assessment on that basis, we normally found that the risk of breaking into any one account was minimal.

But with computer viruses, we known that if somebody breaks into Joe's account, they can insert a virus, and when Mary uses one of Joe's programs Mary will become infected. Anybody that uses Mary's programs thereafter can also become infected, and anybody that uses any of their programs, and so on. So it spreads from place to place to place, and it's range, rather than being 1, is potentially

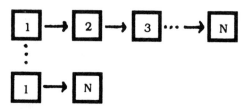

Figure 1.10: The Range Of A Virus

infinite. Think of it in other terms. Sitting at my computer in
Pittsburgh, I could launch a virus and reasonably expect it to spread
through forty percent of the computers in the world in a matter of
weeks. That's dramatically different from what we were dealing with
before viruses.

The third major difference between viruses and everything that
came before them is persistence. This is perhaps the worst part of
the problem. Take for example backups.

It used to be, we thought of backups as our safety net. We also
saw hundreds of articles by so called experts saying "Keeping good
backups will protect you from computer viruses." It's not true.

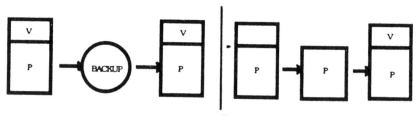

Figure 1.11: Viruses Can Be Persistent

Here's the problem. When you backup an infected program, you
don't just backup the program, you backup the virus. That means
that when you restore from backups, you don't just restore the program, you restore the virus. In other words, the backup acts as safe

harbor for the virus and makes it much more difficult to get a virus out of a system than it would be if you didn't have those backups.

Let me give you some real good examples. Suppose I wrote a virus that only did subtle damage or didn't do any damage for six months. That means you would have six months of backup tapes infected with this virus. When the damage finally happens, you might get rid of the damage and clean your system up by restoring from backups that are say, two weeks old. Well, you've just brought the virus right back, and it's going to hit you again and again. In fact, you don't know how far back into the backups to go to have a clean system. You can never be absolutely certain you've gone back far enough.

But, it gets worse. How about a network with floppy disks on personal computers? If anybody in the network has a floppy disk that's in a desk drawer somewhere, that's a backup. You may have a copy of a virus on that disk. Even though you cleaned the entire network and all the known backups, this one floppy disk sitting in a desk or in a briefcase can bring the virus back into your network, and there you go again. Let me give you a real world example.

There's a virus called the "Scores" that works against MacIntosh computers. I know of several organizations where they've cured the scores virus from hundreds of MacIntosh computers in a network once a week over a period of two years. They keep getting rid of the virus, but it keeps coming back, because somewhere, somebody has a floppy disk made during that week that doesn't get cleaned up. When it is brought back, it brings the infection back.

So this persistence issue is really quite serious and makes getting rid of viruses much more difficult than other attacks. It's even more interesting to note that viruses tend to persist longer than almost anything else in the computing environment. For example, every couple of years you get a new version of a spreadsheet program. If your old spreadsheet program was infected, the new version will eliminate the infection, but because the virus is in the environment, it will eventually infect the new spreadsheet program. So a virus persists beyond changing from generation to generation of software programs.

Eventually, you probably change every piece of software in your computer system, but the virus may still persist. When you go from DOS 2.01 to DOS 2.3, to 3.0, to 3.1 to 3.2 to 4.0 to OS/2, the same viruses that worked on DOS 2.01 almost certainly work on each of these updated operating systems. In fact, if you wrote a computer virus for the IBM 360 in 1965, chances are it would run on every IBM compatible mainframe computer today, because these computers are upward compatible.

1.7   High Risk Activities

What are the high risk activities? Three basic things cause this vulnerability; sharing, programming and changes. All we have to do is eliminate those three things and we are perfectly safe. So does anybody think we are now done with the short course? You mean you want to be able to share information and write programs and change information? Then you're in trouble I guess.

1.8   Summary

Let's quickly summarize. Viruses are programs that replicate, evolve, and/or infect. They spread from program to program, user to user, computer to computer, and network to network. Their unique properties are generality, persistence and extent. It is an integrity problem, not a secrecy problem. Therefore, improving computer security to keep secrets better does not eliminate the virus problem. Similarly, old risk assessment techniques do not apply. Finally, most current systems are extremely vulnerable.

Out of the ten thousand people I've talked to about computer viruses in the last couple of years, we've had three people who claim to be invulnerable to this particular problem, and after great discussions, I find that they are probably right. They are the people who make nuclear missiles. Why aren't they very vulnerable? Because they combine all of the integrity techniques we discuss, sparing no expense. As you will see, you can be almost completely invulnerable, but you have to pay so much that you have to be in the nuclear missile business to justify it.

Chapter 2

Real Viruses

2.1 Some Early Experiments

I would now like to move into a description of some of the early experimental results with computer viruses and then to descriptions of some of the viruses in the real world. I am not going to go into a list of all of the existing viruses, because there are simply too many of them to list, and new ones come up so often, that by the time you publish a list, it is no longer complete. Furthermore, the vast majority of these viruses are not interesting from a scientific point of view, in that they represent no new ideas or technology, and they don't substantially change the problem of defense. Instead, I'm going to go over what I consider to be the more important breakthroughs in viruses so that we can learn about some key issues.

In the beginning, we did experiments. We didn't just say "Let's go play". Experiments where performed to demonstrate feasibility, determine infection time, and help predict attack time. Permission was obtained from systems administrators before each attack. That was to keep me out of jail. Implementation flaws were meticulously avoided. Let me give you an example.

- We did an experiment on a Unix System early on, and one of
  the things that people said was "Yes, but Unix is fundamentally
  weak". For some reason they thought that because you could
  bypass some of the controls in one implementation of Unix,
  that invalidated the reality of viruses. So we did experiments
  on other systems, and always there were those who said "Yes,
  but that system is fundamentally weak". In nearly every virus
  experiment I have ever done, someone has said "that operating
  system is fundamentally weak, so it's not important that you
  can use a virus against it".

The point is, these viruses didn't exploit implementation flaws,
they exploited flaws in the security policy. That is, the policy that
allows you to share information and interpret it in a general purpose
way, allows a virus to spread, regardless of the implementation.

Finally, the National Security Agency in the United States called
me into a meeting one day and said "We don't think it's appropriate to reveal the names of systems that are vulnerable to an attack
until the manufacturers have the chance to eliminate the vulnerability". That means I can never, ever, tell you that I've performed
experiments on Unix, VMS, MVS, TSS, VM, DOS, and many other
operating systems. So, in keeping with their request, I won't tell you
that.

2.1.1   The First Scientific Experiment

The first scientific protection related experiment with a virus was
certainly not the first virus ever to exist, but it was unique in that it
was the first experiment we have found that exploited the infection
property to bypass normal controls. This experiment was conceived

November 3, 1983, performed over the next several days, and demonstrated on November 10th to the attendees of a computer security course.

This experiment was on a *blank* computer, running the *blank* operating system (in keeping with the NSA's request). The purpose was to demonstrate feasibility and measure attack time. It took eight hours to develop by an expert, and was far more complex than any of the viruses we have seen in the real world. Even though this virus was one of the largest I've seen, it was only a 200 line C program (that sort of gives away the operating system doesn't it?), so it wasn't a very big program compared to most other programs in the environment. Most of the complexity was due to precautions we took to assure that it would not spread out of control and that we could trace its spread. It had at least one feature that no other virus since has displayed, as a means of spreading to the largest number of users in the smallest amount of time, it sought to infect the most often used programs first.

Infection time was under 1/2 second in the middle of the day on a heavily loaded timesharing system. So let me just ask: on a heavily loaded time sharing system in the middle of the day, is anybody going to notice a 1/2 second delay in running a program? How about a one second delay? A two second delay? Four seconds? Is anybody going to notice an 8 second delay? Alright, yes. Somewhere between four and eight seconds, there's always a person that says "I'm going to notice that delay." The point is, people don't tend to notice 1/2 second delays under these conditions. Nobody noticed the 1/2 second delay in any of our experiments.

The viruses demonstrated the ability to cross user boundaries, which was the only protection provided on this sort of system. Thus, it bypassed all of the normal protection mechanisms.

There were five attacks launched, and the minimum time to completely take over the system (i.e. the time to attain all access to all information) was five minutes. The average time was thirty minutes, and the longest time in five experiments was one hour. This was somewhat surprising. In fact, at that point in time, I said to myself, "this cannot be true of most systems". I thought that this must have been a fluke having to do with this system, so I wanted to do a lot more experiments to find out about other systems.

2.1.2   A Bell-LaPadula Based System

I really wanted to do instrumentation, because with experiments you can only show what happened in one case, but with instrumentation, you can get good statistics that show you what's going to happen on the average. I tried to get permission for instrumentation, but before I had the chance to do that, I got to do an experiment on a Bell-LaPadula Based System, one of these high-class computer security systems intended to protect from the leakage of secrets.

Negotiations began in March of 1984 and the actual experiments were performed in July of 1984. It was a Proprietary Univac 1108 based system, and I can practically guarantee that you have never encountered it. There were only two copies of this operating system ever in existence, and I heard a few years ago that these systems were decommissioned. I don't remember the name of the operating system, but if I told it to you, it wouldn't have any meaning anyway, and besides, I promised not to tell anyone the name of the site.

The purpose of this experiment was to demonstrate the feasibility of a virus in a Bell-LaPadula based system, and performance simply was not an issue. It took 18 hours to develop by a novice user of both the 1108 and this operating system, with a little bit of help from another user who told me how to use the editor, helped me find the right manuals, etc.

Infection time was a very slow 20 seconds. The virus demonstrated the ability to cross user boundaries and move up security levels. It was an ugly program; 200 lines of Fortran, 10 lines of Assembly and 50 lines of command files. It was a Fortran program that called an assembly routine to run the command interpreter to compile another Fortran program. It was not a glorious example of programming.

So I went to do the demonstration, which was very interesting because I had the Chief of Computer Security for that organization, the Chief of Security for that site, the person that designed the operating system, the programmer who wrote the operating system, and the person in charge of the whole facility at the demonstration. I described what I was going to do, that I was going to launch an attack that showed that the least trusted user on their system could corrupt classified information throughout. Well, the guy that wrote the system said "It's impossible to do that, there's no way". If you ever give a demonstration, there's nothing better than having a guy across the table say that what you're about to do is impossible.

So I did it and he said "Gee, I guess it's not impossible, huh." He asked how I did it, and I described about Bell-LaPadula and moving up security levels, etc., and he got really upset. He said "I don't know why we had you here, you're the worst programmer I have ever seen. In 15 minutes, I could write a program to do this, it would go through the system like a hot knife through butter, and nobody would even notice it." So I said, "that's the point!". Well, he finally got the point.

2.1.3 Instrumentation

We finally got to do instrumentation once on a pair of systems. Negotiations began in April of 1984, and by August, 1984 instrumentation began. It was a *blank* computer again, running the *blank* operating system. It's a very popular operating system. (If you've never used a *blank* computer, you should try it.) The purpose was to confirm or refute the previous results on takeover time, measure attack times, and try to improve protection. It took an expert 8 hours to develop the instrumentation.

Much to our surprise, the minimum time to completely take over the system dropped to 30 seconds. If you got real lucky, and you put the virus in just the right place at just the right time, it would take over the whole system right away. The average however, remained at 30 minutes, and the longest time was about 48 hours.

Originally we couldn't figure out why there was a big clustering of takeover times around 48 hours and 1/2 hour. What we found out was that people logged off the system Friday night and didn't use the system until Sunday evening. On Sunday evening, they all logged in to read their mail, and then they all get infected. So if you launched a virus just after everybody left on Friday, everybody would get infected on Sunday evening.

Another interesting thing we found out was that, if you announce a new program on a bulletin board and that program contains a virus, you can typically take over a computer system in 10 minutes. Anybody want to guess why? It's not that everybody reads the bulletin board and runs the program. One particular person reads the bulletin board and runs the program. Who might that be? The systems administrator. It turns out that if you announce a new program on the bulletin board, within about 10 minutes, the average systems administrator will noticed it and run it; therefore corrupting all of the system files immediately.

In fact, what we found was a set of social users. That is, users that tend to run a lot of other users programs and write programs that a lot of other users run. So, it's just like biological diseases. Viruses tend to spread faster through people that display a lot of social behavior. If you cut down on the way social users do these things, then you can slow the spread of computer viruses in the same way that if you decrease the interactions of social individuals in society, you can slow the spread of biological diseases. We made several suggestions to improve protection, particularly in protecting those social users.

2.1.4 Psychological Effects of Experiments

There are also psychological effects. As soon as we succeeded in launching an attack, other sites said, in effect, "Oh, you mean it works? Well in that case you can't perform any more experiments." In other words, you can only perform an experiment on breaking security if it fails. If it's going to work in demonstrating a vulnerability, people are not interested in it, and that's that. In fact, we couldn't, and still to this day can't, get permission to do instrumentation on systems to try and find out what the average attack time would be or to try and understand how this behavior works.

2.1.5 Experiments We Never Got To Perform

We demonstrated feasibility for a number of systems, but eventually they all refused to allow experiments. Most administrators were unwilling to even allow use of sanitized versions of log tapes. All I can say is it looks like a fear reaction. What we seem to have run into is a situation where once you've violated the sanctity of a computer account, even in an approved experiment, they feel as if they've been personally violated. That is, for somebody that uses a system day-after-day for five or ten years, writing programs, writing papers, keeping notes, etc. there is a very personal feeling about that area of the computer. People feel personally violated when you do things to it, and they react just like victims of assault. So, I guess we should learn how to be survivors instead of victims.

2.2   The Computer Virus Record Book

People tend to be interested in records because they indicate the
end-points of technology. Let me tell you about some of the records
regarding computer viruses.

2.2.1   The Smallest

The record for the smallest virus is a Unix "sh" command script. In
the command interpreter of Unix, you can write a virus that takes
only about 8 characters. So, once you are logged into a Unix system,
you can type an 8 character command, and before too long, the virus
will spread throughout the computer systems of the world. That's
quite small, but it turns out that with 8 characters, the virus can't do
anything but replicate. To get a virus that does interesting damage,
you need around 25 or 30 characters. If you want a virus that evolves,
replicates, and does damage, you need about 4 or 5 lines. In one
of our Unix experiments, we created a 5 line virus that replicates,
evolves, does data diddling damage, and works on just about any
Unix system. It's very easy to write, and you can do it in very few
lines of code.

2.2.2   The Fastest on a PC

Another interesting record is on an IBM PC, that is, a 4 megahertz
processor, 5.25 floppy disks, and no hard disk. It turns out that to
get an infection onto that floppy disk, takes about a half second, just
enough time for the disk to spin around one time.

2.2.3   Spreading in Networks

The first record for spreading on a PC network was established in
1986 or '87, (I believe it was '86) by some graduate students at the

University of Texas at El Paso doing a legitimate and authorized experiment. They wrote a computer virus for a standard IBM PC network using a token ring network architecture. They launched the virus, and within 30 seconds, the virus entered all 60 computers on the network. At this point the students said "Wait a minute, we don't want this virus getting out to the rest of the world, we'd better turn off all those computers." So they literally ran to all 60 of the computers in this relatively small environment and shut the power off.

Well, a couple people were slightly offended. They had been entering data for 4 to 6 hours without saving their entries, when their computers were switched off. The experimenters decided it might be inappropriate to perform further experiments.

That was the network record for a number years, but in 1987, the IBM Christmas card spread, and at its peak, it was replicating at the rate of 500,000 times per hour in mainframes throughout the world. This was according to reports by people at IBM several weeks later, but I've subsequently heard from a gentleman at IBM who is authorized to and probably actually knowns, and he told me that this figure is off by a factor of 10, but he won't tell me whether its high or low.

So somewhere between 50,000 and 5,000,000 copies per hour were being replicated at the peak of the IBM mainframe attack, but that's not the record anymore. The "Internet Virus", at its peak, was replicating in approximately 6,000 computers, approximately 1,000 times per second each. That was 6,000,000 replications per second. So that's the standing record as far as I know, but have heart, I understand that people are working around the world to try and beat that record. You can probably count on it being broken in the next couple of years.

2.2.4   Other Time Dependent Indications of Interest

Some other interesting things; In 1984, there was one researcher, and
there were two papers on viruses. There was one news article, and
it happened to be in the United States. In 1985, Europe had many
news stories and there were two researchers. By 1986, there were
15 researchers. By now there are well over a thousand independent
researchers in this area, thousands of news stories per year, several
hundred people in governments around the world working on this
problem, about thirty people in US universities seriously working on
the problem, and 8 or 9 conferences dedicated to computer viruses
each year

2.3   Real World Computer Viruses

Let me just go down the list of attacks that I consider to be especially worthy of note. The reason I don't go through all the attacks
that have ever taken place is that as of March 1, 1990, the research
community knew of over 125 real world viruses. According to the
IBM high integrity computing laboratory, they were getting a new
virus about every 6 days. These were not new versions of old viruses,
each was a completely new virus. It's infeasible to go through all the
details of all these viruses, and it's also not particularly important
to understand all of the minor variations on a theme to understand
what is going on.

2.3.1   The Lehigh Virus

I am now going to describe in some gory detail what happened at
Lehigh University, after which I will describe what happened with
the virus at the University of Maryland. The reason is that there
are some very dramatic differences between the way they reacted to

these viruses, and their reactions had widespread effects on the rest of the world.

The "Lehigh Virus" was launched in the Fall of 1987. It was probably launched by an undergraduate student at Lehigh University with significant experience with IBM PC computers. It infected the DOS command interpreter (a file called COMMAND.COM) by modifying it to include a routine that infected the first 4 disks it came in contact with, and then destroyed all of the disks currently in the system. The destruction was done by overwriting the "File Allocation Table", which keeps track of the locations of files on the disk. It replicated in the "stack segment" of this program, and as a result, it didn't change the size of COMMAND.COM, but, it did modify the modification date of that file. According to the people at Lehigh University, if it had not changed the modification date, it might not have been found for a much longer time.

The Lehigh virus was detected only as a side effect of the massive damage it unleashed, but in order to really understand this, you have to understand how the environment at Lehigh University operated. As a means of providing site licensed programs to users, Lehigh University had floppy disk libraries. When a student wanted to use one of these programs, they would go into the library, take out the disks, put copies onto one of the PCs in the local site, and use them as required. Many students legitimately made copies to take back to their dorm. When they are done using the software, they return it to the central library.

On a typical day at that central library they have about five disks come in bad. Floppy disks are generally unreliable, especially in an environment like this. Some of them have bit errors, some of them get bent, some of them get dusty, etc. Whatever the cause, about five disks per day go bad.

On this particular day, 500 disks came in bad, so they suspected something was wrong. The user consultants at Lehigh University had been educated in computer viruses (by me, as it turns out), so they were aware of the possibility of a virus, and immediately suspected it. They began to examine these destroyed disks, and they found out that the COMMAND.COM modification date was very recent on many of the disks in the library. They then disassembled COMMAND.COM and compared it to an original copy of DOS that had never been opened (it was in the bottom of a file cabinet), and they found this virus.

By midnight, they figured out how this virus worked. By 4 o'clock the next morning, they wrote a program to detect its presence on a disk and automatically wipe it out. By 8 o'clock the next morning, they had a piece of physical mail in every physical mailbox on campus, electronic mail in every electronic mailbox on campus, and a person with a PC at every outside door on campus. Everybody that entered or left any building was required to put their floppy disks into one of these systems to cure any infections. If they had a PC at home and they needed a copy of the cure for their system, the people at the doors would hand them a copy to take home.

Within two days, they wiped out every single copy of this virus from that environment. That is, no copy of that virus has ever been seen anywhere else in the real-world.

Let me just point out what might have happened if one or two things were a little bit different. Suppose, for example, that the virus had replicated sixteen times instead of four times before doing damage. Then there would have been four times as many copies in the first generation and sixteen times as many copies in the second generation, etc. There would have been many more copies, but they would not have been detected as soon, because the damage would have been delayed longer. They probably would have detected it a day or two later. So, a day or two later doesn't make much difference does it?

Well, it turns out that this virus was detected two days before the Fall vacation at Lehigh University. During Fall break at universities in the United States, most students bring floppy disks home from school to do homework assignments and share software with students from other schools. They usually put this software into their parents' home computer system, and there the problems really begin. The parents typically take floppy disks back and forth to work, so if the infection had entered these machines, it would have moved into thousands of other computers in companies throughout the region. From there, it would have spread on, replicating, and doing massive damage. Instead of the 500 systems at Lehigh University that lost all of their data, we probably would have seen several orders of magnitude more damage.

2.3.2 The Brain Virus

By contrast, let's look at what happened at the University of Maryland where the "Brain Virus" first appeared in the United States. The "Brain Virus" was written by two brothers from Lahore, Pakistan (Ashad and Ahmed according to the copyright notice in the virus - we will probably never know who launched the Lehigh Virus).

When the "Brain Virus" first appeared it didn't do any obvious damage. In fact, the only reason anyone noticed it at first was that it changed the disk label of unlabeled disks to read "(C)BRAIN". The Brain virus changes the "bootblock" of disks, so that when you put an uninfected disk into an infected system, it infects the bootblock of that disk, even if it's not a bootable DOS disk. If you use the newly infected disk to boot another system, that system will also become infected. The only other effects of this virus are that it reduces available memory by a few thousand bytes, it marks several blocks of disk space bad, and uses this space to store itself, and on fairly rare occasion, it causes disk failures.

This virus spread around the University of Maryland unchecked over a period of weeks, and when they had their Fall break, students took it home. Over the next three months, at least a hundred thousand copies are well documented as having appeared and infected systems throughout the world. In this case, there wasn't a big defensive effort. It took several weeks to figure out what was going on, partly because nobody at Maryland knew what a virus was or what the risks were. It spread and spread and spread, and as a result, we may not get rid of all of the copies of the "Brain Virus" for a long time.

2.3.3   The Jerusalem Virus

One of the major controversies surrounding the Hebrew University virus is the question of whether it was launched by a terrorist group or not. A terrorist was suspected because the damage was scheduled to cause widespread destruction of data on the 40th anniversary of the last time there was a Palastinian state.

This particular virus replicated inside binary executable programs in the DOS operating system, but it didn't properly check '.EXE' files prior to infection, so it reinfected the same programs again and again. It was first detected by people with brand-new PCs who started loading software onto their disks, only to find that a 20Mbyte disk was full after being loaded with only about 2Mbytes worth of software. They did a directory and found out that DOS programs had grown to incredible sizes. Eventually, they created a special purpose defense, and got rid of most of the copies, but not all of them. As a result, the Jerusalem virus is still spreading and doing damage in the world today.

2.3.4 The Swiss Amiga Virus

The story of the so-called "Swiss-Amiga Viruses" is interesting for a number of reasons. It is called "Swiss" because someone at first thought it was launched from Switzerland, but the last time I heard of people searching for the source, they thought it was from Germany or Canada. Nothing is quite like closing right in on the source.

To understand how this particular virus works, you have to understand how Amigas work. Not the technical aspects, but rather how people share information when they use Amigas. Amigas have very strong user groups. For example, it's not unusual for an Amiga user group to have a thousand people, with meetings twice a week. So they have several hundred people meeting twice a week, exchanging disks with each other, giving talks, and doing all sorts of social computer related things. Sharing is very prevalent under these circumstances.

This virus enters one of the system files on an Amiga, and eventually destroys the information on the disk in a similar way to the PC based viruses we have discussed. When I first heard about it, I called up the person at Commodore in charge of defending against it; the chief systems programmer. He said "I have it under control, it's no big deal", and he wrote a program that looked for the first byte of the virus in that particular file. If the first byte of that virus was present, it said "this is an infected program, restore from backups to repair the problem" or some such thing.

So, he sent this "defense" out, and about a week later there was a new version of the virus that started with a different first byte. So I called the guy up and said "Wouldn't you like to do something better?" He said "No, no, we have it under control ...", and then he sent out a program that looked for either of those two first bytes. The third round involved a copy of the virus that evolved through any of ten different first bytes, so I called him again and he said "No, no, I've got it under control ..." This time he wrote a program that checked to see whether the first byte was not the legitimate byte of the Amiga program. About a week later, there was a version of the virus that had the same first byte as the legitimate Amiga program, but a different second byte. That was the last time I bothered calling this guy up. I figure that by now, they're up to about the tenth or eleventh byte, and still battling it out.

2.3.5   The Mainframe Christmas Card Virus

In 1987, we also had the mainframe Christmas card virus that spread throughout mainframes of the world in computer mail. It was created by a student in Germany as a Christmas card. In order to understand how this virus worked, you have to understand that part of the corporate culture in IBM was for people to send each other Christmas cards via computer mail. As a result, when someone you knew sent you a Christmas card you would normally read it without hesitation.

So this person in Germany created a Christmas card and sent it to the only two people he knew. The first recipient looked at it and said "I don't know this guy, I'm not going to look at this Christmas card". It was Friday afternoon, and the second recipient went home. On Monday, he came in and read his Christmas card, and it put a fairly poor looking Christmas card on the screen and said "Merry Christmas". But, unbeknownst to the recipient, it also did something else. It looked through his list of outgoing mail recipients (the people he normally sends mail to), and sent a copy of this Christmas card in his name to everybody on that list. Naturally, when they got this Christmas card from their friend, they said "Oh great I'll read it" and they all read it and it sent copies to everybody on their outgoing mailing list, and on and on.

So at it's peak there were something like 500,000 copies per hour.

It brought down most of the computers in the European Research Network (ERN), the IBM internal network (VNET), and the American version of ERN (BITNET). It brought them down for about two hours and then, because of a limit in the network protocol, brought the network down again. For about eight weeks afterwards, they had what the people at IBM called minor "aftershocks". That's when a couple thousand copies appear here or there in the network.

2.3.6 The MacMag Virus

In 1988, the MacMag virus was the first computer virus to be used for advertising purposes, which I guess means that the technology matured. MacMag is a Canadian Magazine for MacIntosh users, and in 1988, they commissioned a professor from a University in the United States to write a computer virus for them. The press, in keeping with the wishes of the computer security community, did not reveal the name of this particular professor, and I understand the professor was rather upset, because he figured this was his way to fame and fortune. The security community took the position that to reveal the name would glorify the attacker, and the press went along this time.

The MacMag virus modified a system file on the Mac II computer so as to put a message on the screen on a particular date saying something like "Happy 2nd Anniversary to the Mac II, our wishes for world peace", and it was signed "MacMag". In order to launch the attack, MacMag placed a copy on CompuServ. CompuServ is one of these service networks in the United States where you can make airline reservations, look up bibliographic database information, etc. You can also store programs there for other people in the network to retrieve if they wish to do so.

Within two days, somebody that picked up a copy of this virus, detected its presence, and notified the people at CompuServ. At about that time, I found out about this attack, so I called up Compu-Serv and said "Gee, would you like some help to get rid of this virus?" They said "No, no, we have it under control.", and they had their favorite contract software house write a special purpose program to delete this virus, announced it on the bulletin board, and told everyone to use it. As punishment, MacMag was kicked off of CompuServ "forever", which I guess is as big a punishment as they can come up with. CompuServ and most of the rest of the community thought the attack was all over, until ...

About two months later (so the story goes), a man was visiting his friend who was a contract programmer. He showed his friend a copy of a game called "Frogger". The programmer tried Frogger once, and said "This is really a dumb game, in fact, this is the dumbest game I've ever seen. I'm never going to run this game again". However, once was enough.

This particular programmer, it just so happens, writes training software for several companies, including such industry leaders as Lotus, Ashton-Tate, and Aldus. Over the next couple of weeks, he distributed copies of his newest training software to some of these companies, and the virus that came in Frogger spread to one or more of them. Aldus subsequently released about 5,000 copies of their newest program "Freehand" which were infected. This was the first time (but not the last time) that a known virus was released in a legitimate, shrink wrapped, commercial software distribution.

2.3.7   The Scores Virus

The so called "Scores" virus operates on Apple MacIntosh comput-ers, and was apparently written by a disgruntled ex-employee of Elec-tronic Data Systems, a Texas firm that does computer security work world-wide. The reason we believe this, is that it directs its attacks against programs written by particular programmers from EDS, and through an anonymous source, I heard some further details that were convincing.

The Scores virus does absolutely nothing for about four days after its initial infection. For the next four days, it infects, but does no other damage. The 4 day time period may be because of a procedural defense at EDS, which a 4 day wait bypasses, but nobody is certain of this except the attacker. From then on, whenever you run an infected program, it operates as follows:

- For the first 15 minutes of operation it does nothing.

- For the next 15 minutes of operation, it does not allow the user to save anything.

- Finally, the system crashes.

So if you are running an editor written by one of these authors at EDS, for the first 15 minutes everything works great. After that, when you try to save the file, it says (in effect) "Sorry, I can't save that". The user typically responds with something like "What do you mean you can't save it? Save it!", and for the next several minutes, a frantic effort to save the file is made, until finally the system crashes, and the changes are lost. Needless to say, it is a very disconcerting experience for the user when it happens the first time, but things get worse ...

It takes about 2 hours to completely get rid of the Scores virus from a MacIntosh with a hard disk (from the details I have heard), but and as I have mentioned, there is another side effect. Over the four day period of replication without damage, the virus tends to get into many floppy disks, spread over networks, etc. As a result, virtually no organization that has had the Scores virus has been able to completely eradicate it.

2.3.8   The Internet Virus

The "Internet Virus", commonly called the "Internet Worm" (it turns out that worms are a special case of viruses), was launched in 1988 in the Internet. The Internet is a network that interconnects about 100,000 to 200,000 computers around the world, is used by Universities and other research organizations, and provides connectivity to many other networks. I can't remember the names of half the networks it is connected to, but among them were the ARPA-net (Advanced Research Projects Agency) and the DOD-net (US Department of Defense).

In the Internet attack, a graduate student at Cornell University, designed and launched a computer virus which replicated and moved from machine to machine in the Internet. It entered about 60,000 to 70,000 computers, but was designed to only replicate in 6,000 of them. In a matter of a few hours, it spread throughout the network causing widespread denial of services. It was not designed to deny services, but due to an error in programming it replicated too quickly.

It was designed specifically to work in a particular version of a particular operating system and, even though it would be very simple to make it work on other versions, special code was in place to prevent its undue spread. It replicated by 'fork'ing processes and tried to move from system to system by exploiting a bug in the computer mail protocol. It turned out that if you had debugging turned on in the mail protocol on your machine, then if somebody wanted to, they could issue commands as if they were the Superuser on your computer. It also turns out that most of the systems in the Internet had this switch turned on at compile time, and in many cases, they could not turn it off because they didn't have the source code to the mail program for recompilation.

This particular virus also crossed the boundaries between the ARPA-net and the DOD-net, which were supposedly secured against all such intrusions. In the next few days, several viruses apparently crossed this boundary, and the link was then severed.

2.3.9   The AIDS Disk

In late 1989, a well funded group purchased a mailing list from a PC magazine, and distributed between 20,000 and 30,000 copies of an infected disk to the people on this list. The disk was a very poor virus, but it caused a great deal of damage because there were so many copies mailed, and the recipients used the disk widely despite the policies in place prohibiting such use.

The disk was advertised as a program to evaluate a person's risk of getting AIDS based on their behavior. Included in the distribution was a description of the fact that this was a limited use distribution, and that it would cause damage to the system if it was used without paying royalties.

The disk infected the host system by adding a line to the "AU-TOEXEC.BAT" system startup file which, although it appeared to be a comment, was actually a peculiar program name. After running this program a number of times, the virus would encrypt directory information so that file names became unusable. If you continued to use the system it would eventually try to convince you to put in a floppy disk to make a copy for a friend.

The alleged perpetrator was eventually caught by tracing the mailing list purchase process back to the buyer.

2.3.10   The Datacrime Virus

The "Datacrime" virus was the most widely announced and least widely spread well known virus in recent memory. It was rumored to exist as early as 6 months before it was to cause damage, and was eventually the subject of the first NIST National Computer Virus

Alert in the United States. This virus only caused minor damage in
a few instances in Europe, and never took hold in the United States.

2.3.11   The Evolutionary Virus

In late 1989, the first seriously evolutionary virus to appear in the
real world began spreading in Europe. Earlier viruses had evolved
in minor ways, simple self-encryption had been used before, and experimental viruses with no association between evolutions had been
demonstrated, but this virus was the first one to be released into the
world with many of these properties.

This virus replicated by inserting a pseudo-random number of
extra bytes into a decryption algorithm that in turn decrypted the
remainder of the virus stored in memory. The net effect was that
there is no common sequence of more than a few bytes between two
successive infections. This has two major implications. The first
problem is that it makes false positives high for pattern matching
defenses looking for the static pattern of this virus, and the second
problem is that special purpose detection mechanisms were simply
not designed to handle this sort of attack.

2.3.12   The Simulation Virus

The simulation virus that appeared in late 1989 represented a major
step toward attacks meant to bypass virus defenses. In essence, this
virus simulates all of the DOS system calls that would lead to its
detection, causing them to return the information that would be
attained if the attack were not present. It is presently spreading
widely throughout the world, and because it does no obvious damage,
it is generally going undetected.

2.3.13   The Bulgarian Viruses

In early 1990, a research institute in Bulgaria released a set of 24 Bulgarian viruses that had not previously been known outside of Bulgaria to the world research community. Astonishingly, none of these had been detected in Western Europe until these samples were provided.

Chapter 3

Sound Technical Defenses

There are three and only three things you can ever do to absolutely and perfectly prevent a computer virus from spreading throughout a computer system or network; limit sharing, limit transitivity, or limit programming. This has been proven mathematically.

3.1 Limited Sharing

The first thing you can do is limit sharing. So let me give you an example of what we mean by limited sharing. Here we have a Bell-LaPadula based system where a user at a given secrecy level cannot read information that's more highly classified, lest it might be leaked to them, and they can't write information to an area that's less classified, lest they could leak information out.

Similarly we have the Biba Integrity Model. If you are at a given integrity level, you can't read information of lower integrity, less it might corrupt you, and you can't write information of higher integrity, less you might corrupt it.

If you want both secrecy and integrity, all you have to do is

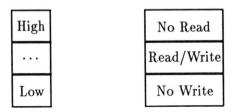

Figure 3.1: The Bell LaPadula Security Model

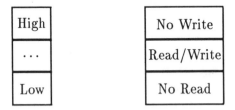

Figure 3.2: The Biba Integrity Model

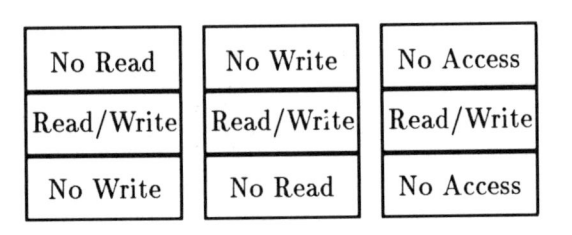

Figure 3.3: Combining Secrecy with Integrity

eliminate all the sharing, since as you can see, putting these systems together yields a system in which you cannot read or write up or down.

It turns out that this is only one specific case of limiting sharing. Let me show you what you can do more generally to limit sharing. The best you can ever do (i.e. the most general structure for limiting sharing, in a general purpose transitive information network with sharing), is to implement a policy based on a structure called a POset, a partially ordered set.

Mathematically, a partially ordered set follows these rules:

$\forall$ 'domains' A, B, and $C \in$ the POset.

1. $A \le B$ and $B \le C \to A \le C$

2. $A \le B$ and $B \le A \to A \le B$

3. $A \le A$

Basically, a POset can be pictured as a bunch of boxes with lines between them, and a rule that says information can only flow up (or left to right if you turn it on its side) Here's how it works.

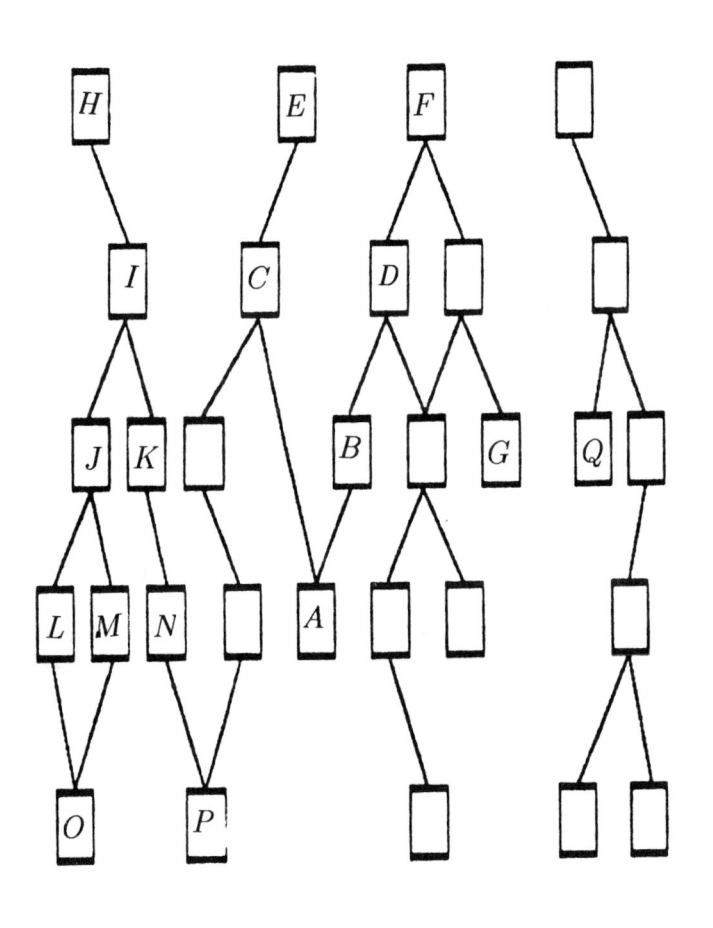

Figure 3.4: A POset

Suppose somebody in *A* writes a computer virus. Well, let's see, it could spread to *B*, *C*, *D*, *E*, and *F*, but it could not spread to *G*, because there is no path for any information in *A* to ever get to *G*. If no information in *A* can ever get to *G*, then no virus in *A* can ever get to *G*.

Similarly, if somebody in *H* is trying to leak information, they could potentially leak information from *I*, *J*, *K*, *L*, *M*, *N*, *O*, and *P*, but they could never leak any information from *Q*, because there is no path for information in *Q* to ever get to *H*.

In other words, we are limiting the flow of information, and the most general structure for doing this is a POset. So let me put this into more familiar terms by using this example, a picture of a POset that describes some of the operation of a typical business.

You might get *letters* in the *mail*. The *letters* might generate *orders* or *payments*, and if they generate *orders*, that generates *shipping* and *invoicing*. *invoicing* and *shipping* go to the *customer*. *shipping* and *invoicing* copies also go to *file1*. When a *payment* comes in, it gets mixed with *file1* to generate a *deposit*, the *payments* independently generate a *commission*. That's how information flows through some parts of this organization.

What we can then do is associate individuals with these areas. Say Joe is a programmer who works in *letters*, Mary programs in *file1*, Jill programs in *shipping*, etc, etc, etc. So we assign individuals to the operational aspects of each of those areas and we have thus structured the flow of information in our organization. Let me point out some advantages of this technique.

One of the advantages is that if somebody launches a virus, it only spreads to a subset of the organization. For example, if Joe launches a virus from *letters*, it could potentially get to *letters*, *orders*, *payments*, *purchase orders*, *questions* and *bills*, and then indirectly from there to *payments*, *file1*, *approval*, *commissions*, *deposit*, *file2*, *invoice*, *shipping*, and *customers*. It could not get to any of the other

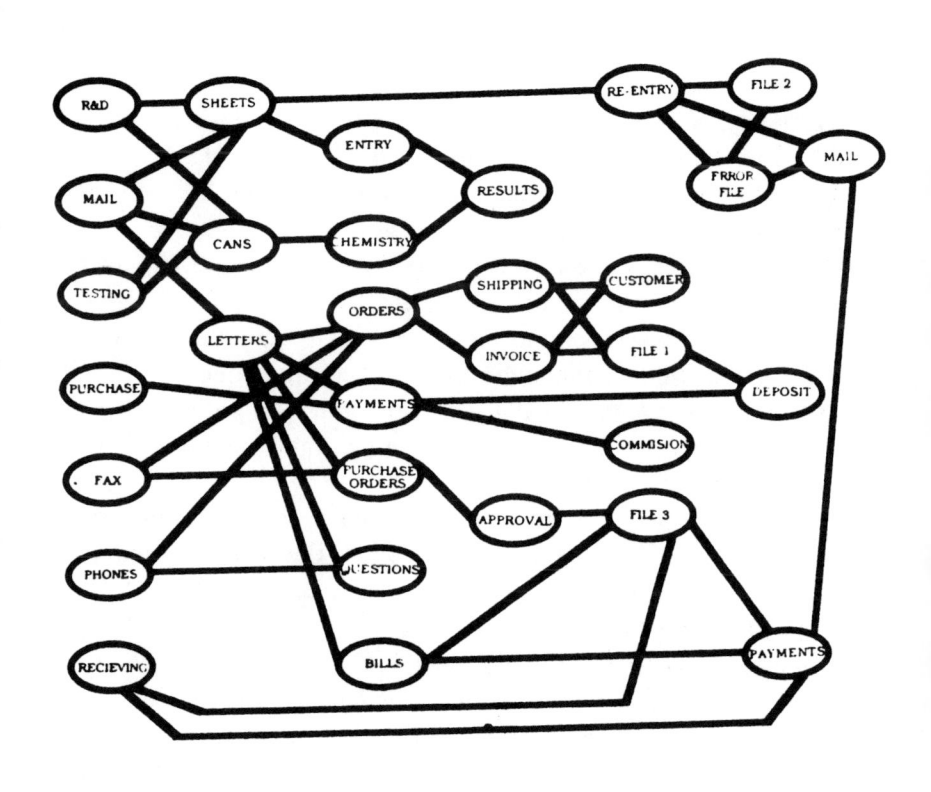

Figure 3.5: An Example Business's POset

domains, so the entire organization is not vulnerable.

But there is more to it than that. Suppose we somehow find that there are things going wrong in *shipping, customers, file1,* and *deposits,* and we suspect it is a virus. Where could that virus have come from? *orders?*

If it came from *orders,* it would probably also get to *invoicing.* Therefore, it probably didn't come from *orders.* Could it have come from *invoices?* No! It could not have gotten from *invoices* to *shipping.* We have isolated it very quickly to *shipping.* In other words, structuring the flow of information allows us to track down the sources of corruption efficiently.

Similarly, we can track down where information might be leaked. For example, if we are getting information leaks from *shipping, invoice,* and *customer,* the only place that could have leaked that information is *customer.*

So this structuring, besides limiting the ability of viruses to spread and limiting the ability to leak information, also allows us to track down the possible sources of corruptions and leaks.

There are some other significant advantages to this approach to protection, in that it substantially reduces the complexity associated with protection management, and it makes the implications of protection decisions immediately evident. For example, a POset based protection system for a typical timesharing system has only a few hundred bits of protection information, while a standard timesharing system has on the order of 1,000,000 bits of protection information. Just as a side note, this type of system has been successfully prototyped, is in use in a couple of organizations, and it's becoming more popular.

3.2   Limited Transitivity

The second of three possibilities for absolute prevention is limited transitivity. Here's how it works.

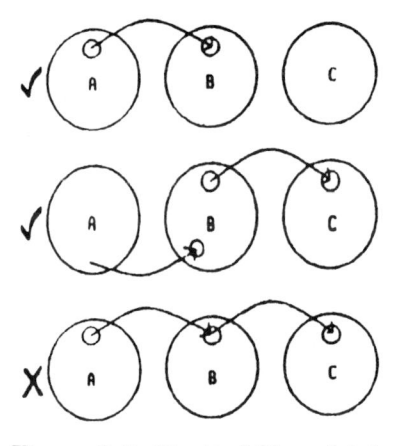

Figure 3.6: Limited Transitivity

A might be able to give information to B. In fact, A could give information to B and B could give information to C. But it's against the rules for A to give information to B which B then passes on to C. For example, if A writes a virus it could get to B. But if A wrote a virus that got to B, it could not be passed on to C.

If you can implement limited transitivity you can prevent a virus from spreading more than a certain distance from its origin. The only problem is there is no feasible way to use this in a real computer system. It is feasible to implement limited transitivity, but when you try to use it, almost everything spreads as far as it can spread very quickly, and then sharing is almost entirely halted. The problem is that viruses are just like any other information, so whatever you do to restrict viruses has to apply to all other information as well.

3.3 Limited Function

The third of three possibilities for absolute prevention of computer viruses in a computer system or network is limited function. Here's how that works.

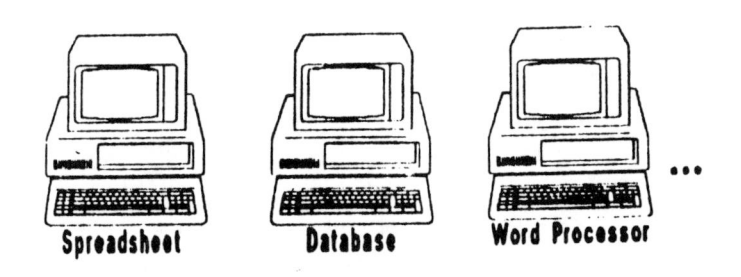

Figure 3.7: Limited Function

We could, for example, have a system that allows you to enter data into a database, selectively put it into a spreadsheet, analyze it, put the results into a pie chart, pass the pie chart to a word processor, and print the result in two column format in color on a laser printer. We can do all of that without giving users general purpose functions.

Unfortunately, today you can't buy a database that doesn't have database macros allowing general purpose function. So you can write a database macro that replicates and spreads from database to database. In fact, you can write a database macro to infect databases and spreadsheets. Similarly, you can't buy a spreadsheet today that's any good, without having spreadsheet macros such that the user can enter a macro that spreads from spreadsheet to spreadsheet, or from spreadsheet to database, or even over to word processors. Similarly,

word processors have macros that tend to be general purpose, so it's fairly straight forward to write a word processor macro that spreads from document to document.

There are some situations where we do have limited function in the real world. For example, most EFT (Electronic Funds Transfer) networks are limited in their function. The way EFT networks normally operate, any information on the network is treated as a *from* account, a *to* account, an *amount* of money, and a *check* string. It doesn't matter what you put in that network; you can send a basic program, and the network will treat the first so many bytes as *from*, the next so many bytes as *to*, the next so many bytes as *amount*, and the next so many bytes as *check*. If *check* doesn't match, the network will ignore the transaction and report it as an error.

The reason you can't infect one of those networks is not because the information being sent over the network doesn't contain viruses. It's because no matter what information you send over that network, it cannot be interpreted so as to replicate. In other words, the limited function does not come from the information, but how it's interpreted. Let's think of it another way. Information only has meaning in that it's interpreted. So unless you interpret it with a method that allows it's meaning to be a virus, you can't have viruses. That's what we mean by limited function.

Now many of you may have menu systems for your secretaries and data entry people, and you may think they are limited in function, but they aren't necessarily. Let me give you an example.

I was at a computer conference in California in 1985, and for one reason or another, my invitation included the proviso that I had to evaluate all of the computer security systems at this conference. I was only provided with an expert programmer (a high school student that could tell you which bits to deposit into which locations in memory to modify the operating system to do whatever you wanted). So I walked around to the first booth, where I came across a limited

function interface. I asked if I could do a little experiment to see if we could break into their system, and they said:

> "There is no way you are going to break into this system. It's absolutely safe."

I said:

> "Really?!?, that's great, then you shouldn't mind a little experiment, right?"

So they gave me the least privileged account they could. This was an account that was only supposed to let you store a file on the system or retrieve that file back. That was all you could do with this account. So I said okay, let's try it. I went over to the expert and I asked for the name of the user login 'profile' file that describes how the system first interacts with the user upon login. I told the system to store into that file. The system obliged, and stored a command to run the system command interpreter in that file.

Low and behold, the next time we logged in, instead of putting us into the limited function interface, it put us into the command interpreter, and because the designers were so sure that this was limited function, they didn't provide any of the normal operating system protection. We were logged in with Superuser privileges.

So we walked over to the next booth, and by the time we got there, the guy at the second booth said "Don't bother, it will work against our system too". We went to the 3rd and 4th booths, and they said the same thing. Just because it says "limited function", doesn't necessarily make it so.

Chapter 4

Defenses That Fail

So those are the three and only three things you can do for absolute prevention, and given that you are able and willing to do those things, you can limit the ability of viruses to spread in a computer system or network. If those are inadequate for your needs, you might like to look at other types of defenses, in particular; detection and cure.

These defenses are all in the class of imperfect defenses, so we can't expect perfection, but we have a couple of questions we might like to ask about what you can and cannot do to get an idea of what is likely to work and what is likely not to work. So let me introduce a couple of issues:

- Can we write a program to look at other programs and tell whether or not they have viruses in them?

- Suppose we have a sequence of instructions that we have identified as a virus. Can we write a program to find all of the infections that can result from it?

- Is there a statistical method for detection? Maybe we can put some sort of statistical mechanism on our system that identifies

viruses when particular behavior takes place.

- If we find a virus, can we remove it? More specifically, can we remove it without shutting down the whole system?

- I'll tell you the story of the Thompson C Compiler.

- We will discuss Complexity Based Integrity Maintenance Mechanisms, otherwise known as "Software 'HAYA'! Self-Defense". Yes... Computer Karate. Programs that defend themselves.

- We will then talk about N-version programming, user awareness, vaccines, instrumentation, and so on. But what I'll tell you right now is that these defenses leave us in a position of "survival of the fittest", and we are currently in a situation where the attackers seem to be much more fit then most of the defenders.

4.1   Can We Detect Viruses?

Is this program CV a computer virus?

```
Program CV :=
  { ...
  main-program:=
    {if D(CV) then goto next;
     else infect-executable;
    }
  }
next:
  }
```

Suppose you had somebody that wrote a program D to detect computer viruses. It would look at any other program P and return

TRUE if P was a computer virus and FALSE if P was not. So let's take a look. See program D being called from CV? If your program says CV is a virus, then CV will not infect an executable. So if D says CV is a virus, then it is not. But if D says that CV is not a virus, it infects an executable, and is thus a virus. So no matter what your detection procedure D says, it's guaranteed to always be wrong.

That means you cannot write a program D, which correctly determines whether or not another program is a virus, unless that program:

- runs forever without a result in some cases -OR-

- has an infinite number of false positives (things it falsely identifies as viruses) -OR-

- has an infinite number of false negatives (things that it does not detect as viruses, even though they are viruses) -OR-

- has combinations of these three problems.

4.2 Can We Find Resulting Infections

Let's go a step further. Suppose we have a known program 'EV', and we have determined that EV is definitely a virus. The question is, if we have some other program, say EV_2, can we write a program D', that looks at EV and EV_2 and tells whether EV_2 is an evolution of EV, and therefore, whether EV_2 is also a virus?

```
Program EV:=                Program EV2:=
  {...                        {...
  main-program:=              main-program:=
    {if D'(EV,EV2)              {if D'(EV2,EV)
      then goto next;            then goto next;
      else infect-exec          else infect-exec
          with EV2;                 with EV;
    }                          }
next:                       next:
  }                           }
```

Well, let's take a look. Decision procedure D' is suppose to tell us whether EV evolves into EV_2. If D' says EV does not evolve into EV_2, then EV evolves into EV_2. If your program says that EV does evolve into EV_2, then EV does not evolve into EV_2. So again, you cannot determine in general, all of the evolutions of a known virus. At least not systematically with a program.

Let me clarify this, because it is a bit obscure in mathematical form, and I want to put it into as solid a basis as I can. I'm going to do that with an example. We have here an example of an evolutionary virus and I'm going to tell you how it works.

At time $t = t_0$, we have a program P_1 that is infected with this particular virus and a clean program P_2. If, at time $t = t_1$, we run P_1, the following steps take place.

1. First D_1, a decryption algorithm, decrypts V_{c_1}, the encrypted version of V, into the original V.

2. Second, V is run.

3. V selects a different encryption algorithm E, re-encrypts itself with E_2, giving us V_{c_2}, and places a decryption algorithm D_2

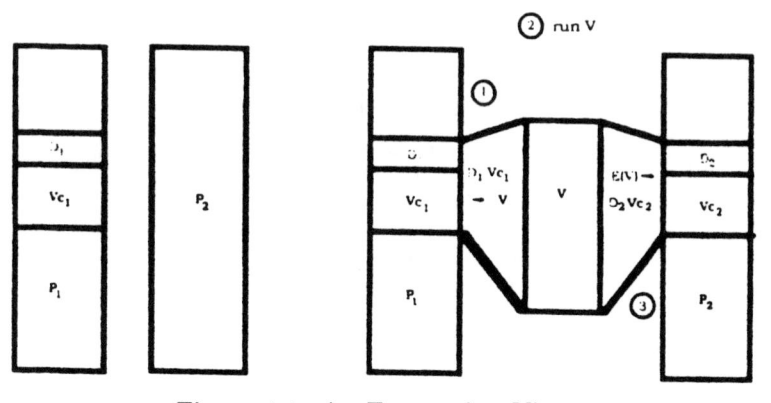

Figure 4.1: An Encryption Virus

(designed to decrypt things encrypted with E_2) into program P_2 along with V_{c_2}.

Excepting the probability of random sequences coinciding, no common sequence of bytes exists between P_1 and P_2 due to this virus.

Let me give a more specific example, suppose V_{c_1} was encrypted with a DES encryption. When we run P_1, D_1 decrypts V_{c_1} using the DES to get the original virus V. Then virus V chooses the RSA crypto-system and encrypts itself with the RSA, leaving V_{c_2}. It then puts an RSA decryption algorithm D_2 along with V_{c_2} in program P_2. So what do you say, does anybody here think that they are going to be able to write a program to automatically, given any D_1 and V_{c_1}, figure out that D_2 and V_{c_2} are an evolution of it? Does anybody see even a little hope for doing this automatically?

Well, if you thought that was bad, you haven't seen anything yet!

We have here, a new version of that evolutionary virus, where V has a whole set of encryption algorithms ($E_1 \ldots E_m$), decryption algorithms ($D_1 \ldots D_m$), triggering mechanisms ($T_1 \ldots T_m$), infection

EVEN WORSE ! ! !

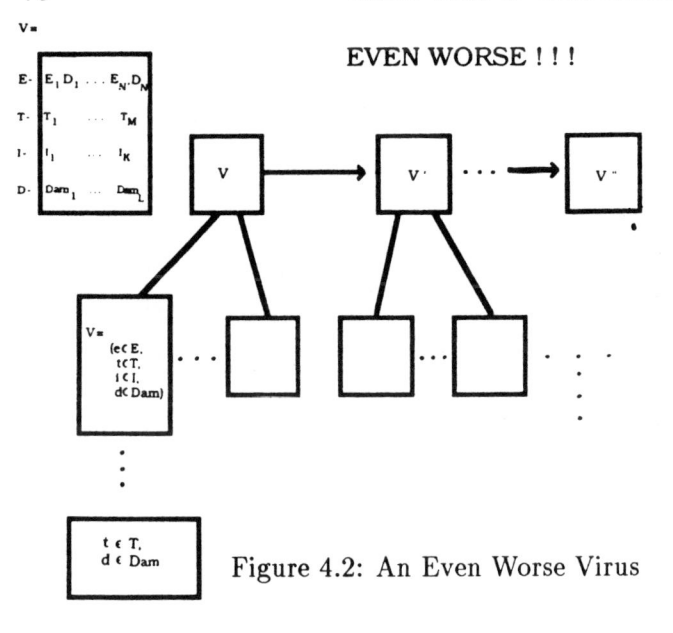

Figure 4.2: An Even Worse Virus

mechanisms $(I_1 \ldots I_m)$, and damage mechanisms $(\square_1 \ldots \square_m)$.

We have already mentioned two encryption algorithms, and there are certainly thousands more that can be automatically generated. There are also key-customized algorithms that can be automatically generated.

Triggering mechanisms might include a wide variety of time, use, and logical conditions, perhaps generated pseudo-randomly from a large class of such algorithms. Infection might include such variations as "put it at the beginning of the file", "put it at the end of the file", "put it in a bootblock", "put it 23 instructions from the beginning", "put it 25 instructions before the middle of the program", "put it at a pseudo-random 'return from subroutine' statement", etc.

A large number of damage mechanisms are also easily generated. For example, "change the 5th bit in the 7th byte of the program", "change the 25th through the 29th byte in the 7th program you find",

"look for data files with the 123 extension, and modify the first cell in the spreadsheet", etc.

The virus evolves and spreads through programs in your computer system for a while just as the evolutionary virus above, but then it replaces itself with a subset of the encryption and decryption algorithms, triggering conditions, infection mechanisms, and damage mechanisms. It then repeats the whole process, spreading and evolving for a while, then replacing itself with a subset, etc. As time goes on, you may have a very wide variety of different variations, all looking very different from each other in terms of the sequence of the bytes that appear in your system, and spread throughout your computer and backup systems.

One day, you will start having minor damage; a file gets deleted, oh maybe some bits get changed in a random data file. Suppose you identify those things right away, you work real hard, and you figure out which Trojan horse caused the damage. You search your entire system and you find no other copies of that Trojan horse, so you figure you're safe. About five minutes later, two things start to go wrong, then three, then four, then five. Over the next couple of days, you probably get to the point where hundreds of thousands of these simple things are starting to go off in all sorts of ways.

So what do you do? You go to your backups, right? You go back a week in the backups, you search for all these different patterns and you find none of them. There is no indication that anything there is corrupt, but it starts happening again. You go back two weeks, three weeks, four. You go back as far as you want, there is never any way to be sure that this isn't happening again. This points out the problem with evolution, the problem of tracking down viruses once they are throughout a system, etc.

Several questions usually come up here. For example: "How you keep these from reinfecting the same program repeatedly?" You don't have to of course, but there are a variety of ways to limit

infections. For example, never infect anything larger than a given size, or with a modification date ending in the digits 1,2,or 3. Some of the examples later will point this out more clearly, but let it suffice to say that no universal recognition mechanism is necessary in order to operate such a virus successfully.

4.3   The Tail Chasing Problem

The tail chasing problem comes when you try to remove a virus from a system while that system is in active operation.

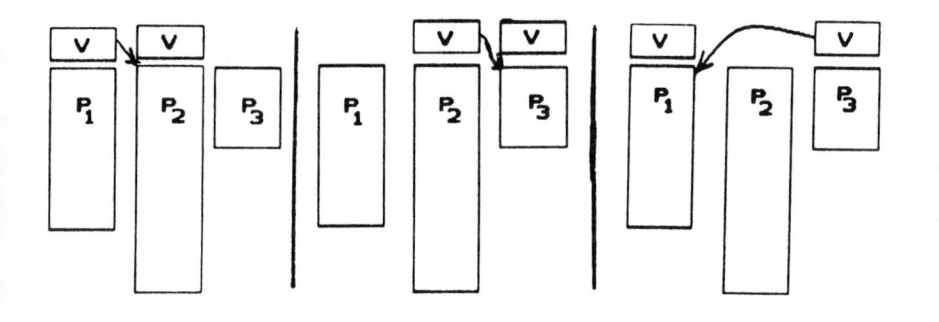

Figure 4.3: The Tail Chasing Problem

Suppose we have an infected system, and it's operating as we are detecting and eradicating viruses. In this example, P_1 and P_2 are infected. When we detect a virus in program P_1 we cure it, but in the meanwhile, P_2 is run and it infects program P_3. No problem, we find that P_2 is infected and cure P_2, but in the meanwhile someone runs program P_3, which goes and reinfects program P_1! We are now chasing our own tail.

Whether almost everything is almost always infected, or whether almost everything is almost always clean, depends on the relative rates of infection and cure. This follows the biological theory of epidemics. Basically, the number of infected programs times the frequency of use gives the number of new infections per time. If this exceeds the rate of cure, then the chances are that almost all programs will always be infected. If the rate of cure exceeds the rate of new infection, as time goes on, the system will become completely devoid of infected programs.

Under certain conditions, you can even get an equilibrium situation. As an example, when the number of already infected programs slows the infection rate to near the cure rate, more cures will cause more infections, while fewer cures will cause fewer infections, and thus we may be in a stable condition.

Currently, our cures, except in the rarest cases, are very slow. Our viruses on the other hands, are very fast. So for the most part, in current situations, it's rational to deny services while performing cure. There are some advantages in a well structured system. For example, in a POset network, once a virus is detected, we know the extent of where it could have come from and gone to, and thus, which portions of the system may be operated unhindered while cure is performed. So you don't have to deny services to the whole system, you just deny services to those areas that might be affected.

There is one well known computer security consultant in the United States that says: "If you get a virus, the first thing you should do, is turn off your computer and call in an expert". Of course he is a consultant, so he is one of the experts you might call in.

4.4   The Thompson C Compiler

Ken Thompson, a very well known researcher, won the Turing award
in 1984, and in his honorary speech, he described a modification
he had made to the Unix C Compiler, purportedly for the National
Security Agency Computer Security Center (which was recently shut
down by a presidential order).

He made a minor modification to the Unix C compiler to add
a special feature. If you compiled a copy of the login program for
Unix, it would modify it in compilation to allow Thompson to login
to your system. Some people may ask "Suppose you compiled the
C compiler again, then you would have a clean C compiler, and you
could compile the login program". But Thompson was more clever,
he also modified the C compiler so that when you compile a new
C compiler, it propagates the bug. In other words, compile a clean
login, you get a dirty login. Compile a clean C Compiler, you get a
dirty C Compiler. In still other words, Thompson can log into your
system.

What makes this even more dangerous is that almost every C
compiler ever written is probably based on one of Thompson's original C compilers. That is, people usually don't write compilers from
scratch, they write compilers using other compilers. They compile
the new compiler using the old one, and eventually they have their
own C compiler, which they use from then on. So if Thompson did a
good job of this, every C compiler in the world today would probably
have this bug.

I figured out how to get around this. You write a funny looking C
compiler and compile it with this dirty C compiler. What you get is
a maybe clean version of the C Compiler. It might be clean because
Thompson's C compiler may not be able to figure out that this is
a C compiler. In fact, the more poorly written this funny looking
C compiler is, the less likely it is to be recognized by that dirty C

compiler. Conclusion? For high integrity, get a lousy programmer. Somebody who can write a C compiler that is so poorly written, that nobody and nothing (including Thompson's C compiler) could figure out it's a C compiler.

4.5 Instrumentation

Viruses are normal-user programs. That means that whatever statistic you use to determine whether something is a virus, it's always possible for a virus to slip below it if other programs can be written to slip below it. As you lower the threshold to try to catch viruses, eventually you will lower it enough to catch some legitimate software, and then you have a choice.

- You can throw it away, in which case, if it had a virus, you eliminated that copy of the virus, but you also threw out the program. If it was legitimate, you just threw out a legitimate piece of software, and you still don't know if you are safe. So you keep lowering the threshold, throwing out more and more software, until you are completely safe. All you have to do is throw out all your software. Then your system is completely safe, but it is also useless.

- You can decide to trust it because it is an important program. But if you decide to trust it and it has a virus in it, you've just trusted the virus and therefore allowed it to continue to exist in your system.

- There is only one other possibility. When you detect a possible infection, you determine whether or not it is actually infected. So how do you do that? Well, we have already shown that it's undecidable to tell whether a program is infected. In other

words, trying to look at it to tell whether it's infected doesn't work, because you can't ever be sure one way or the other.

That's why instrumentation has problems. Instrumentation comes down to verifying all the software in your computer system, which we cannot do. By the way, that doesn't mean that you should not ever use instrumentation. For example, you could reasonably have a set of normal operating parameters on your system, detect when the system goes outside those parameters, and take appropriate action. It just isn't perfect.

4.6   Vaccines

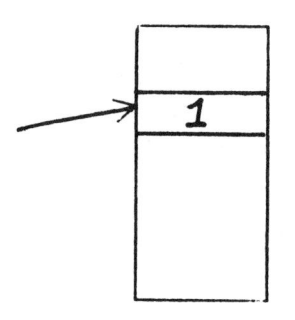

Figure 4.4: A Vaccine

If you have a virus that looks for itself in another program and does not infect the other program if it has already been infected, then the vaccine might fake the indicator used to determine whether the program has already been infected. Let me point out some problems with this.

The first problem is that, in order to be effective, you have to vaccinate against a large number of viruses. In other words, you have to go and modify your existing, executable programs to have

all of the various indicators of the (now over 125) known viruses, and every six days, if you want to keep up to date, you have to modify these programs again to include the new indicators. Perhaps there is a 1 at location 8 and a 7 at location 15 for one of the viruses, and a 12 at location 3 for another virus, and so on. If you try and do that to your programs, it's going to be very difficult to keep your programs working.

The second problem is that not all viruses can be vaccinated against. For example, the Jerusalem virus cannot be vaccinated against because it doesn't look to determine if programs have already been infected. Even for some of the vaccinable viruses, vaccination might be quite expensive. For example, suppose we have a virus that only infects programs smaller than 30K bytes. Small programs would have to be made large in order to prevent infection, thus dramatically increasing disk usage. This may be the only side effect of the virus, and thus we are doing more damage by defending in this way than the virus causes in the worst case.

The third problem is that vaccinating against one virus may permit another virus to enter. This comes from the concept of competing pairs in the population.

Suppose we have virus V_1 which works like this:

- If location 4 is less than or equal to 24, do an infection.

The vaccine is to make location 4 greater than 24, so that V_1 will not infect a given file. But suppose we have another virus V_2 that works like this:

- If location 4 is greater than 24, do an infection.

To counter V_2, we have to make location 4 less than or equal to 24. Since you cannot make location 4 less than or equal to 24 and also greater than 24, you cannot vaccinate against both. By sending this pair of viruses out, vaccinating against one of them only reduces the

occurrence of that one in the population, and thus provides more food for the other virus. If you vaccinate against V_1, you increase the population of V_2 because you are providing a lot of food for it. V_2 eats all the new food, but as V_2 eats more and more, it provides more food for V_1. The system eventually returns to a stable population ratio.

4.7   Virus Scanners

A Virus Scanner is a program that examines systems for the occurrence of known viruses. Modern virus scanners are very fast. They can typically scan 3 Mbytes worth of executable programs for 100 or more viruses in only about 4 minutes. They are therefore sometimes used as a bootup check for known viruses in personal computers. They have some major problems that make them expensive and ineffective in most circumstances, even though they are currently very popular in the marketplace.

The first problem is that they are only good against known viruses and other known attack patterns, so they won't work against a virus that the organization did not know about ahead of time.

The second problem is that they tend to take a noticeable amount of time to scan a system or network for these patterns. In a normal PC based installation, a scanner that looks for 100 known viruses takes about 4 minutes at bootup. If this is done throughout a large organization on a daily basis, it costs about $1 per day per system, or about $250 per year per system.

The third problem is that in order to remain effective, a scanner must be updated often. Otherwise, by the time you detect a relatively new virus, it will have spread throughout your organization, and you will have a massive cleanup problem on your hands. Suppose you only update 4 times per year, and the cost of sending out and

installing an update is $5 per copy. That comes to another $20 per system per year.

The fourth problem is that scanners are not very good against evolutionary viruses, some of which have begun to appear in the real world recently. Even some non-evolutionary viruses may be quite difficult to scan for, since they may place themselves in a non-fixed location in the infected program. The speed of current scanners comes mostly from knowing where to look in a file for a known virus. If they have to scan entire files for known patterns, they become very slow, taking over 5 minutes per megabyte. This is also why scanners are ineffective against viruses in non-executable programs. These programs (e.g. spread-sheets, data-bases, etc) don't typically store the virus in a fixed location.

The fifth problem is that they produce false positives for short patterns. That is, they tend to indicate the presence of some viruses when that virus, in fact, is not present. It is not unusual for a new version of a program to have a pattern similar to a known virus in it, and for several scanners to begin indicating false positives in response to a program update.

4.8 Software Self Defense

The idea of self-correcting code came up a number of years back. Basically, it works by having a program examine itself and automatically removes the corruption. The object is to have a program with some redundancy built into it. When you run the program, it checks itself using that redundancy, and if it isn't normal, it detects the error and corrects it, again using the redundancy to assist in correction. There are a couple of problems with this scheme.

The first problem is that the virus may modify the redundant part of the program P_1 to accept or even propagate the virus. Here's

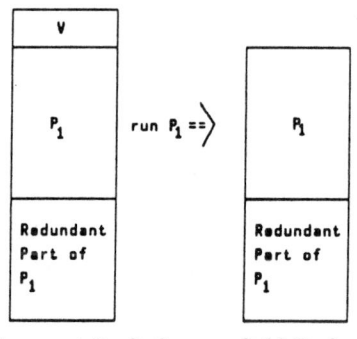

Figure 4.5: Software Self Defense

an example:

- There's a program called "Mirror" that runs on the PC. Mirror makes an exact copy of a program, except that all the ones are changed to zeros and all the zeros are changed to ones, and stores the mirror image on disk. Whenever you run the program, the operating system compares the original to the mirror image. If they aren't exactly opposite, it mirrors the mirror image to give you a clean original.

- Somebody wrote a virus that infects the mirror image with a mirror image of the virus. When you run the program, the system compares the original to the mirror. They disagree, and the mirror image is mirrored, giving a new, cleanly infected version of the program.

The second problem is that detection may fail. If you use a simple checksum, we have already shown you how to make that fail with a compression virus. If you use the size and modification time or a CRC code, or any combination of those, it's the same thing.

There are a lot of other things that product designers do to try to increase performance while compromising as little protection as

possible. One of them is to do a cryptographic checksum that only checks the first and last block of a file. Another is to only check the header information of a file. Some select five or six blocks from the file to check, or some such thing. There are all sorts of schemes to make checking very fast by not checking all the information, but they tend to fail.

The third major problem is that by the time the program gets ahold of itself, it may look clean. It turns out this is really the death blow to self defense. Let's see why that is.

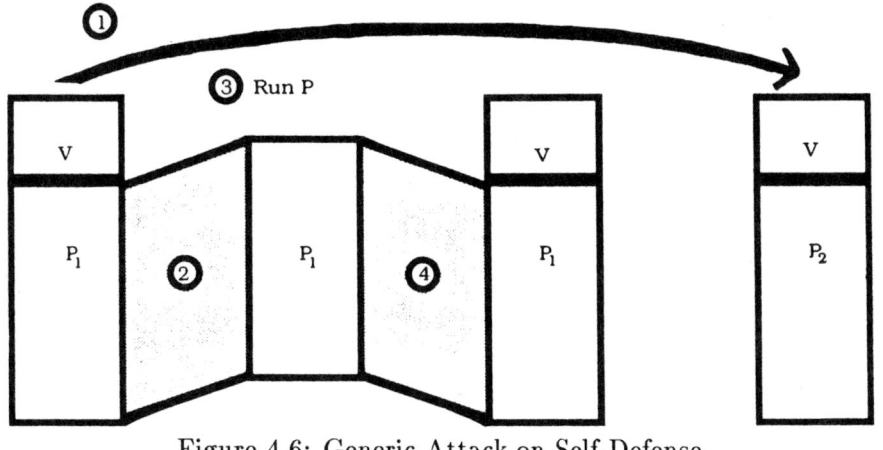

Figure 4.6: Generic Attack on Self-Defense

Here's a generic attack against any self-defense mechanism. It's generic in that, if you launch this attack without knowing what self-defense the defenders are using, only that it's a self-defense technique, it's guaranteed that this attack will work. One attack fits all.

Initially the infected version P_1' of program P_1 is infected with the virus V, and the clean version of the program P_2 is uninfected. If at time t_1, we run P_1', the following sequence of events takes place:

1. V infects some other program P_2.

2. V replaces P_1' with the original P_1.

3. V runs the original P_1.

4. After P_1 finishes, V replaces P_1 with P_1'.

During step 3, P_1 looks at itself and determines that it is clean, because indeed it is clean by the time it is run. The same thing can be done by simulating the operating system call where P_1 looks at itself. Both of these situations have occured, the first in a laboratory experiment, and the second in the real world.

Chapter 5

Solid Technical Defenses

The defenses we will now discuss are "solid" in the sense that they provide a very high degree of protection, but they are not "sound" in that they do not make viruses mathematically impossible. One of the defenses we will discuss (the "Integrity Shell") is completely practical in the current environment, while the other two have some rather serious limitations that make them inapplicable for all but the rarest of circumstances.

5.1   Software Fault Tolerance

Software fault tolerance is the software version of hardware fault tolerance. Let me give you an example. On the United States Space Shuttle when they enter the atmosphere, this thing is going awfully fast. It is going way faster than the speed of sound, and to slow down, they go through a series of hypersonic S-curves, slowing down so they don't burn up in the atmosphere.

It turns out that during those hypersonic S curves, the shuttle is dynamically unstable. That is, if the computer system that controls

the space shuttle stops working for more than one millisecond, the shuttle will crash and burn, and there is no way any person or computer can recover after that one millisecond of failure. The shuttle will flip over, the wings will fall off, the back will come off, and it will crash and burn.

So what they do, is use redundancy, because they know that computers fail, especially when you are shaking them madly and they are at high temperature, and things like that. They have five computer systems connected together to work like this:

- Three of them vote with each other.

- If one of the three disagrees with the other two, they kick the bad one out and insert the fourth computer in its place. They then again have three computers voting on every instruction execution.

- If one of those fails, they kick that one out, and then the remaining two vote against each other.

- If these two disagree with each other, they are both thrown out, and the fifth computer is used in their place.

The reason they go to the fifth computer is that it is running a different program for the same task, so if a software bug is causing the failures, this computer will not have the same bug. The first time they ran the shuttle, several computers failed.

Well, you can do the same thing in software as you can do in hardware. You can have redundant copies of programs. So here is an example.

We have here a picture of a system with three programs, P_1V_1, P_1V_2, and P_1V_3. P_1V_1 is infected with a virus, and therefore, produces wrong output under some circumstances. Since the output

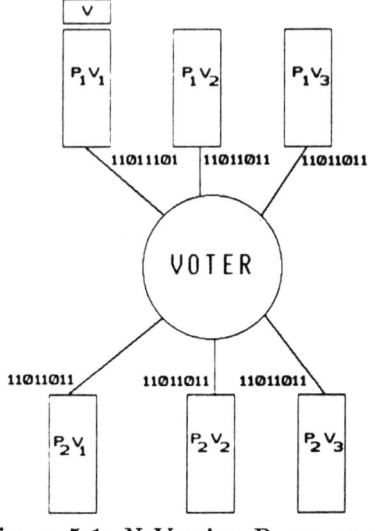

Figure 5.1: N-Version Programming

goes through a voter, when this happens, the voter disregards the bad output, making all three outputs identical, and the system continues unhindered. Thus P_2V_1, P_2V_2, and P_2V_3 all get correct inputs, even though P_1V_1 produces wrong results. The voter is also redundant to cover voter errors. So what are the problems with N-version programming?

- It's expensive. It takes three times the number of computer programs, therefore three times the number of computer programmers. Also, you need three times the computing power to get the same performance. So it is somewhat more than three times as expensive to write a redundant program as it is to write a single program, and that's quite expensive. The high expense means it only applies in rare circumstances like the space shuttle.

- It's hard to do. How hard is it? Well, there was an experiment

done in the early 1980's at UCLA. The experiment involved 100 computer programmers who had just passed a programming course. They were all asked to write a program to add a column of numbers together. Every one of those programs worked, but no two of them worked the same. Let me give you an example:

- Suppose we have an overflow level of 100 and we are adding 75, −60, and 75 together. If we first add 75 and 75, we get an overflow. When we then subtract 60, we may have a meaningless answer. But if we add them in another order (e.g. $75 − 60 = 15$, followed by $15 + 75 = 90$), there is no overflow, and we get the correct answer.

  A great deal of work has been done since this experiment, and we now know that improved specification, verification, and testing is vital to getting N-Version programs to work. More work is underway as of this writing, and the cost of N-version programming is coming down, but it is not yet cost effective for most applications

- This defense is not guaranteed against intentional attack. That is, this defense will work well if the problem comes from random Gaussian noise, but it may not apply to an intentional attack. An intentional attacker, for example, might use the legitimate modification mechanism to modify both P_1V_1 and P_1V_2. Then the voter would kick out the results from version 3. So this defense, at least in this simple form, it's not guaranteed against intentional attack.

5.2 Sound Change Control

Sound change control is a quality assurance process that keeps corruptions from passing a "guard". Normally, we have two environ-

ments, a "Research and Development" (R&D) environment, and a "Production" (P) environment. The R&D environment is where we make and test out changes. The P environment is where we actually use those changes day to day. So how do we do sound change control? ...Very poorly for the most part (sic).

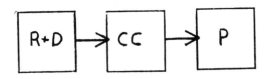

Figure 5.2: Change Control

There's an area between R&D and P called "Change Control", and a set of rules about how the system works. These rules are typically supported by technical safeguards and administrative controls. The rules for sound change control usually go something like this:

1. Change Control can only approve or reject a proposed change; it cannot make a change on its own. In other words, you make changes in R&D and pass them through Change Control. All Change Control can do is say, "This is acceptable!" -OR- "This is not acceptable".

2. Change Control can only pass sources from R&D to P. It cannot pass binary libraries, executables, or other such things, because we can't reliably determine what non-source programs do.

3. Change control is done via human and automated verification methods. What do we verify about them?

   - We verify that the change is necessary. That is, we don't just allow changes to take place for no reason.

   - We verify that the change is appropriate to the goal. In other words, we say we need a change for a particular reason, and we have to make sure that the change relates to that reason.

4. The change has to be tested on sample data from the P environment to make certain it works properly.

5. The operation of the change must be clear and obvious. Unclear and inobvious software can usually be easily modified to include subtle attacks

6. The change may not have any unnecessary code or data involved. Any unnecessary code or data might contain viruses or other corruptions, and is expensive to handle.

That reminds me, does anybody here use change control in their environment? Do you do it this way? No. I've done a pretty thorough survey, and I only know of about three places in the world that do sound change control. One of them is the people that design nuclear missile control systems. I am very pleased that they do sound change control. Another one is the Federal Reserve Bank in the United States. At least they claim to do sound change control. There are probably a few others that do this, but I am sure there are very few.

Why doesn't everybody else do this? There are four major problems with sound change control that keep it from being used in most environments, even those where some form of change control is used.

1. It's quite expensive. According to the places that really do it, you need twice as many people doing change control as programmers making changes, so it triples programming costs.

2. It's quite slow. If you have a serious problem in your computer system, you can't just go and fix it, you have to go through change control. You have to fix it, test it out, show that it's appropriate, and make sure that it is just what it's suppose to be. Then the change goes into affect, and not before.

3. It's rarely done right. As you may note from my informal survey of several thousand organizations, almost nobody follows all the rules all the time.

4. Sound change control must cover all changes! If we only cover changes to the things that are compiled into binary executables, that's not good enough. We have to cover changes to spreadsheets, databases, other macro processors, and all sorts of other things. Everything that isn't limited function has to be change controlled, and this, of course, is intolerable. Almost nobody can afford to do this properly.

5.3 Practical Solutions Today

There are currently very few practical solutions to the computer virus problem, and only one is really practical in both the short and long run. That solution is the so-called "integrity shell".

An integrity shell uses redundancy to detect changes, and is thus a form of automated fault tolerance and change control. We know just when to check and what to check, and we can even, in certain cases, do automated correction. So let's look at how this works.

We begin by restating the problems with software self defense, because integrity shells came about by fixing all of the problems with self-defense techniques. There were three problems:

1. A virus may modify the redundant part of the program.

2. Detection may fail.

3. By the time a program gets control, it may look clean.

5.3.1   A Sound Cryptographic Checksum

The first and second problems have to do with the fact that we need a reliable way to detect corruption in the presence of intentional attack. The only way we know how to do that is with a hard-to-forge cryptographic checksum (for brevity, we will henceforth use the notation $\sqrt{\sum}$ to represent "cryptographic checksum"). So what's that?

I'll start with the checksum. It's like a fingerprint. We take a fingerprint of a file. If we subsequently modify the file, it's fingerprint changes. So when we look at the file the next time, it will have the wrong fingerprint, and therefore we will detect the change. But, we still have to do the fingerprint in a reliable and uncircumventable fashion.

So imagine that we do a $\sqrt{\sum}$ by encrypting the file using a secret key, and then performing a checksum on the encrypted file. If the crypto-system is good enough, and the key is kept secret, we have a hard-to-forge finger print. To be more precise, we have a set of triples $[(F_1, k, S_1) \ldots (F_N, k, S_N)]$, where each F is a file, k is the user specific secret key, and each S is a $\sqrt{\sum}$. Only the user knows the key, while the attacker can see the file and the $\sqrt{\sum}$.

If the crypto-system is "good enough", you cannot modify F so that under the same k you get the same $\sqrt{\sum}$, you can't modify F and $\sqrt{\sum}$ so that under the same k they will match, and you cannot guess k by looking at F and $\sqrt{\sum}$. That's what makes it a sound $\sqrt{\sum}$ technique for this particular purpose.

It turns out that there are a couple of techniques like this that seem to be very good, and the cryptographic community has analyzed these to a certain extent. Let me take a moment to list some of the other properties of $\sqrt{\sum}$ techniques, so we can understand their virtues.

- The $\sqrt{\sum}$ can be independent of the operating system. That is, we can have a $\sqrt{\sum}$ so that even if the operating system is modified by an attacker, even if a system's manager, a system's operator, and/or a system's programmer, collude to make the system work differently without telling anyone, a $\sqrt{\sum}$ can still pick up the change.

- A $\sqrt{\sum}$ is also independent of other users, so that each user can independently verify change control. Each user can have a different key, so that even if an attacker can make a forgery that works properly under one key, it is unlikely to work under all the other keys in the system.

- Multiple, independent checks are possible with $\sqrt{\sum}$. That means that not only can we do internal checking, but an external auditor can come in and do a change control audit and detect what has changed, even though we may not know that it is changed. They can come in and use their own $\sqrt{\sum}$ with complete independence.

- A $\sqrt{\sum}$ can work on all information, not just binary executable files. They can also work on overlay files, database files, data files, or any other sort of information in a computer system or network.

- A $\sqrt{\sum}$ can work over networks. You can do a $\sqrt{\sum}$ on a PC and verify its propriety on a mainframe. You can verify the integrity of information during network transmission, storage, and retrieval, and you can use the same $\sqrt{\sum}$ technique, regardless of the system it's used on.

- There is a tradeoff between performance and protection. We can usually get better protection by sacrificing some performance. That doesn't mean that lower performance always gives you better protection. For example, you might have a slow cryptosystem that isn't particularly good. Nevertheless, you can typically improve the level of protection by using a larger key, storing a larger $\sqrt{\sum}$, etc.

5.3.2   An Integrity Shell

The last problem with software self-defense was that, by the time a program gets control, it may look clean. Recall that there is a generic attack against any self-defense mechanism. How do we get around that problem? The only solution is to check the program before it gets control. We do that using something called an integrity shell. Here's how an integrity shell works:

```
The User says ''Interpret X'':
    If X is unchanged -AND-
        everything X depends on is unchanged
    then interpret X
    else
      - Accept
      - Trust
      - Forget
      - Restore
```

Let's start by describing what I mean by interpreting X. I don't mean that X is an executable binary program that is run on the hardware, although that is an example of interpretation. It might be that I have a spreadsheet which is interpreted by a spreadsheet program. The spreadsheet is interpreted, but it depends for its proper interpretation on the spreadsheet program. The spreadsheet program may in turn depend on a variety of other information. The same is true for a source program that is translated by a compiler or interpreted by an interpreter, a database that is interpreted by a database program, etc.

When the user says "interpret X", if X is not changed, (that is, if the $\sqrt{\sum}$ for X has not changed) and everything X depends on for its proper operation has not changed (that is, their $\sqrt{\sum}$s have not changed), then we know that we have an unchanged environment. In other words the environment has not been corrupted since the last time it was $\sqrt{\sum}$ed. So we can simply interpret X with a reasonable degree of assurance that it is what it is suppose to be.

If either the information being interpreted or the information it depends on for its interpretation has been modified, we cannot trust that the interpretation will operate properly. In this case, we have choices to make:

- One option is to "accept it" in its new form. That is to say, use it, even though you know it is corrupt. For example, if I am on the space shuttle and I am going through hypersonic S-curves and I find a corruption in a program, and it's on my last computer, I don't want to shutdown the computer because it has a corruption, because then I will certainly crash. I would much prefer to run the program until I land (If I land), and fix it then.

- Another option is to "trust the change". For example, if I just made a legitimate change, I would want to tell the system that this change was appropriate, and have it identify further change afterwards. This is often the case during program development and maintenance.

- Another option is to "forget it". For example, if I'm in the nuclear missile business, and I send a nuclear missile out, and the program to control that nuclear missile goes bad, and that corruption is detected by the system, I personally would make the decision: "Don't blow up, fall to the ground, turn off the engine, don't blow up!". This is called "fail-safe" because it fails in a "safe" mode.

- The last option is "restore it". If I have a backup and I know where it is, I can go and get that backup and automatically restore the corrupt information to its previous state. In this case, the system fixes the corruption and proceeds normally with just a slight delay.

5.3.3   An (Almost) Live Demonstration

At this point, in a short course, we normally demonstrate an integrity shell operating with a number of different types of corruption. We begin by turning off integrity protection so we can show a virus as it would operate without integrity present. It spreads from program to program, displaying its progress along the way. We then turn integrity protection back on and repeat the demonstration, only this time, the corruption is detected immediately, and further spread is prevented. Demonstrations are normally done on a portable DOS based system, but they are fairly generic and do not depend on DOS features or limits in any significant way.

Now most of these examples are against viruses, but it turns out that integrity shells don't work only against computer viruses, they are very general purpose mechanisms. Let's look at an example.

We go into the DOS directory, where all of the DOS programs are stored, and we find a program called "FORMAT.COM", which is an operating system program. We run FORMAT to show how it appears on the screen, and then we exit without doing anything of any interest.

```
C:>FORMAT A:
Insert new diskette for drive A:
and strike ENTER when ready^C
```

The next thing we do is type a command like:

```
C:>ECHO No way Jose > FORMAT.COM
```

This replaces the contents of FORMAT.COM. We then type FORMAT.COM to show that it has indeed been corrupted, and do a directory which shows that FORMAT.COM is only 17 bytes long.

```
C:>TYPE FORMAT.COM
No way Jose
C:>DIR FORMAT.COM
FORMAT   COM      17  3-01-89  12:01p
C:>
```

In the DOS environment, if you ran such a program (and I wouldn't advise you to do it without an integrity shell in place), the system would normally crash. That is because the operating system simply loads the file into memory and starts executing instructions at the first byte of the file. So let's run FORMAT.

```
C:>FORMAT A:
Insert new diskette for drive A:
and strike ENTER when ready^C
```

The integrity shell detected the corruption, replaced FORMAT.COM using an online backup, and ran the corrected FORMAT program, taking only a few extra seconds.

If you want to restore from an on-line backup, you need to have the backup on-line. You can do the same thing with off-line backups, but it takes a lot longer. Thus, you get a time/space tradeoff. On-line backups take more space, while off-line backups take more time.

5.3.4   Integrity Shell Limitations

I want to point out the features and limitations of integrity shells. They are pretty good against viruses, but they do have their limitations.

A "Good Enough" Cryptosystem

The first limitation is that the cryptographic system must be "good enough". So what does "good enough" mean? Well, what it really means is that no attacker will get around it, and that's not very easy to predict ahead of time. But, there are some other issues that may be considered. For example, the performance versus integrity tradeoff. Let me give you an example from the integrity shell we use in our demonstrations. It has different cryptosystems depending on how you want that tradeoff placed. So, you have to be able to decide whether you want it to take 10 seconds, 1 second, 0.1 seconds, or 0.01 seconds to check the average program. If you take 0.01 seconds, you're not likely to get much in the way of integrity. If you take 100 seconds, it's probably going to be too slow to justify. So normally, you set a performance level, and do the best you can do for that performance.

You need a sound basis for believability of any cryptographic system. For example, many people come to me and say, "we have a great cryptographic system, it's been approved by the NSA. It must be great." I usually say "Approved for what?" If they say it's been approved for selling overseas, that means the NSA can break it, right? Cryptosystems are usually not approved for export unless the NSA can read them. So you need a basis for believability, and in terms of cryptography, there are only three systems in general use which are credible at this time.

One of them is the perfect system (A.K.A. The One Time Pad), analyzed by Shannon in the 1940's. It is provably unbreakable, but it is not practical for the integrity shell application.

The second cryptosystem that is relatively sound, and I use the word "relatively" loosely, is the DES. This system withstood a fair amount of attack, and although I have heard from several governments around the world that they are able to break DES codes in a matter of days (or in some cases hours), the typical attacker is not likely to break DES codes in order to launch a virus, and if they did, it would take a long time to perform an infection.

The third system is the RSA. In the RSA system, we can break any code, but the amount of time it takes to break the code can be varied by changing the key size. For example, a hundred digit RSA takes hundreds of years to break using the fastest algorithms on the fastest supercomputers. A two hundred digit RSA signature takes hundreds of trillions of life times of the universe to break with the best systems available today, but it also takes more time to generate signatures.

How do you determine whether a system is sound? It's very difficult to determine whether a cryptosystem is sound, but there are some indicators of unsound systems. For example, if you have a cryptographic system that doesn't take longer to check things that are bigger, chances are it's not checking everything, because it takes more time to encrypt more information. There are a couple of products that check 50Kbyte files in a tenth of a second on a PC-XT.

This is certainly not sound, because it takes over a second to read 50Kbytes on a typical PC-XT. Another example of unsound cryptographic practice is the use of an unchangeable cryptosystem key. If we all have the same key, the attacker has it too, and can forge modifications without a problem.

A Trusted Mechanism

The second limit is that the mechanism itself has to be unalterable. If you can't secure the mechanism, an attacker can modify it to allow corruptions to pass unnoticed. You can use the $\sqrt{\sum}$ to check the integrity shell, but if we can alter the mechanism, we can bypass any defense.

In virtually every system, there is a way to use hardware protection to defend the integrity mechanism. Even on a PC, you can have hardware write protected floppy disks that provide a fair degree of hardware protection against corrupting the integrity mechanism. You run an integrity check from the floppy disk to check the integrity mechanism on the hard disk, the operating system on the hard disk, and all the other critical parts of the operating environment, and then you have some assurance that they are sound. You can then start to use them as a basis for running other programs on the system.

Let me just mention something about write protect tabs on PC floppy disks. If you protect a floppy disk with a black plastic write-protect tab, it might not work. It turns out that many PC's use infrared to detect the presence of a write-protect tab, and those little black stickers don't block infrared light. So even though you use the write-protect tab, the disk may not actually be write protected. So you might say "let's get all metal stickers", which we certainly should do, but even with a metal sticker, the disk isn't always write protected properly. On some systems, a little metal finger comes down to check for the presence of a write protect tab. If the write protect tab gets a little bit dented, the disk drive may not detect it. Microfloppy disks, by the way, don't have these problems.

A Trusted Path For The Key

The third thing we need is a trusted path for the key. If the attacker can watch the key as we type it in, they can use that key to forge a $\sqrt{\sum}$. Normally, a trusted path is generated by forcing the integrity shell to run before other programs in the environment, so that nothing can insert itself between the system startup and the integrity shell's operation.

The Granularity Issue

The fourth limitation is really more of a tradeoff than anything else. It's called the granularity issue. If we are trying to cover a 500 megabyte database, and we check the whole database every time we read, and resum it every time we make a change, it gets a little bit painful. For things like large databases, it's probably much more appropriate to have checking at a lower granularity level than the file level. In that case, you would like to have the database program verify the $\sqrt{\sum}$ associated with each record as it is read, and update the $\sqrt{\sum}$ every time a record is written. It is not adequate in all cases to use a command interpreter based integrity shell. In fact, anything that interprets something else, should really have built-in integrity protection.

The Problem Of Intent

The final limitation of integrity shells is a fundamental issue, in that the legitimacy of change is a function of intent. That is, we can't tell whether a change is legitimate or not, unless we can somehow determine what the intent of the user is, and compare that intent to the actual change. In most current systems, most users don't know what part of the system should change when they make a change to something on their screen. They have no sense of that. So ultimately, we have no way to assure the legitimacy of the change in any such system. Integrity shells can detect change and act as they are told, but they cannot determine the intent of the user and map that into the actions of the system.

5.3.5   Integrity Shell Features

Now that we have discussed the limitations of integrity shells, we should also discuss their three main features. They are optimal for defense against viruses in an untrusted computing environment, they are efficient in terms of the overhead required for their operation, and they are highly reliable against both known and unknown attacks.

Optimal Protection

The basic feature of an integrity shell, and the reason the integrity shell was devised the way it was, is that it is optimal. That is, in an untrusted computer system, by definition, you can not prevent infection. Since you cannot prevent infection, the best you can hope to do is to detect it and limit its further spread. That's just what an integrity shell does.

- An integrity shell detects all primary infection (infection by a trusted program), and prevents all secondary infection (further infection by a program infected through primary infection). Furthermore, this is the best we can ever do in such a system.

Efficiency

The second feature of integrity shells is that they are very efficient. When I say efficient, I mean that for optimal protection, integrity shells use the minimum overhead:

- They don't perform any checks that don't have to performed in order to prevent secondary infection, and they only check the things that have to be checked when they have to be checked. So, they are efficient in the sense of minimal overhead.

- They are also efficient in the sense that they can automate the repair process. Without this automation, the costs of getting rid of a virus once found is potentially enormous. For example, if you have 5,000 computers and a virus spreads throughout your organization, you will have a Herculean task cleaning them up. With automated cure, you don't even have to interpose yourself in the process. It is completely automatic and transparent.

- Finally, they are efficient because they are easy to use. That is, from the standpoint of a user, integrity shells can be transparent if you automate all the decisions based on your policy.

I want to mention one other thing about this optimal situation. Some people use a $\sqrt{\sum}$ without an integrity shell. For example, they might perform a $\sqrt{\sum}$ to detect changes every morning. The problem with that scheme, and one of the reasons integrity shells are optimal and this is not, is that a virus could be designed to only infect programs modified in the last day. In this case, only legitimate looking changes would be picked up by the $\sqrt{\sum}$, and the virus would spread undetected. That is why an integrity shell must check information just before use, and automatically resum it after use if there are legitimate changes. It shuts the window for illicit changes being treated as legitimate. There is, by the way, a real-world virus that works this way.

Reliability

Finally, integrity shells are very reliable if used throughout an organization.

- Integrity shells are capable of covering all information, even spreadsheets, databases, and so on. Whatever information you want to check for changes can be covered with an integrity shell because it can be covered with a $\sqrt{\sum}$.

- We can have multiple independent checks so that even if one of the copies of the integrity shell is corrupted, the independent checks will pick it up. It would be very difficult, if not impossible, to forge a modification that is invariant under all of the possible keys of a reasonably good $\sqrt{\sum}$ system.

- They work over networks because the $\sqrt{\sum}$ works over networks. We can write an integrity shell for a file server and have the integrity information passed over the network transparently to the systems being served.

- They even work across different machines, because the $\sqrt{\sum}$ is a mathematical transform that can be implemented on any machine. You can have capabilities to move a spreadsheet from one machine to another, and if they both have integrity shells, even though they are different computer systems with different operating systems, you can still assure integrity over the whole process.

5.3.6 Product Issues in Integrity Shells

There are three major product issues in the design of integrity shells.

Basic Capabilities: Some systems have on-line backup capabilities, others do not. The soundness of the $\sqrt{\sum}$ is vital to proper operation of an integrity shell. Other features are required in various environments, and their existence and quality are critical to the value of the product.

User Interfaces: You probably need a different interface for the systems administrator than for a typical secretary. Integrity shell capabilities must be able to integrate into existing interfaces as easily and transparently as possible, and be relatively easy to deal with. For example, an interface that doesn't integrate with a windowing environment is inappropriate if that is the dominant environment, since it will not be effective most of the time.

Automated Decision Making: Because there are so many different ways to use integrity shells in different environments, and because different decisions are appropriate under different conditions, it is appropriate that decisions be configurable for the environment. A typical issue is whether we should automatically trust new programs in the environment in order to make new program installation simple, or prevent running new software to keep from trusting a program that should not be trusted. Automation should help automate organizational policy to as large an extent as possible.

5.3.7 Future Developments

The major things we lack now are more comprehensive tools for refining the automation of integrity maintenance. We would like to have a language for expected behavior so that, for example, if we have a spreadsheet that's suppose to modify other spreadsheets with the same first three characters of the first name, the process of checking and summing can be automated.

A language that specifies intent is not as simple as it may sound. The closer we can get to specifying our intent, the better job we can do at determining whether our intent has been met or not, but that also implies that we have to know a lot about the way systems work and be able to impart that knowledge to the computer effectively.

Another problem with trying to describe intent is that it is different for different environments, uses, and people. We cannot automatically figure out what's intended. We can get close however, and the closer we get, the less of a difference there's going to be between the actual intent and the specified intent, and the smaller the window of vulnerability we will have.

Chapter 6

Selecting Technical Defenses

In selecting an appropriate defense, many things should be considered, and we certainly cannot tell you about all of them here. They tend to vary from organization to organization, and person to person. We have collected what we consider to be the major issues in technical defenses against viruses, and describe them here to add to the list of things to be considered.

6.1 General Principles

First and foremost, selecting the appropriate defense is an issue of tradeoffs. No single defense is safest for all situations, and no combination of defenses is cost effective in all environments. This underscores a basic protection principle. *Protection is something you do, not something you buy.*

What do I mean when I say that? Suppose we want to protect our house from water damage. It doesn't matter how good a roof we buy for our house, it's not going to protect our house forever. We have to maintain the roof to keep the water out. It's the same with protecting information systems. You can't buy it, you have to do it.

6.1.1   Tools

You need tools to protect your house. For example, you need a hammer to fix the roof when shingles fall off. It's the same with information systems. Protection products are technical tools to help you in that protection activity. To the extent that you decide to use these tools, it's appropriate to consider certain things about them. For example:

- When a large organization buys from a smaller one, it's not unusual to require sources in order to assure continued service. The small company usually doesn't want to give up its trade secrets, and since there aren't any large companies with credible virus defenses at this time, this is a dilemma. One of the more popular ways of dealing with this problem is to move into a software escrow situation, where a neutral third party takes possession of the sources, and only release them under contractually agreed circumstances.

- Technical support is one of the most important aspects of selecting a protection product, because you don't just buy it and ignore it; protection is something you do. The vendor should support what you do. Your environment changes; different parts of your environment have different needs; in the maintenance phase, attacks have to be analyzed, even if they are automatically repaired; you have to be able to maintain integrity as you move to new machines; etc.

- Attackers continue to do research and development to come up with better and better attacks, so it's probably appropriate that the defenders have active research and development to work toward better defensive tools.

6.1.2 Perfect Defenses

There are no perfect defenses, other than limited sharing, limited function, and limited transitivity. When a salesperson comes up to you and says "I have the perfect defense, it protects against all viruses, and you only have to type 'INSTALL' and you are done.", you should probably go to another vendor. Unfortunately, "if it sounds too good to be true, it probably is."

6.1.3 Don't Buy From Fear

Let me give you a story of some people buying from fear instead of a realistic assessment of tradeoffs. When the Internet virus hit, there were a whole bunch of people that bought PC defense products. The Internet virus operated against Unix systems in a Unix network. It had nothing to do with PC's, and yet all these people rushed off to buy the first PC defense they could find. That doesn't make sense. They bought anything they could find, and it probably wasn't a very good defense. Now, they have that lousy defense installed, they know it's no good, and they don't want to buy anything else because they figure all the defenses are no good, or they would have to admit they made a mistake, or some such thing. It's not that all the defenses are bad, it's that you have to think before you buy.

6.1.4 Find Trustworthy Sources

There was an evaluation by one of the big CPA firms of anti-virus products, and they evaluated a broad range of defenses. They were evaluating one of them that did cryptographic checksums and it detected changes on the system. They said, "Hey, our system is not suppose to be changing. We were just trying to see how it operates in our environment. We don't have any viruses here." The people that made the integrity shell said "This is a cryptographic checksum, if it says there was a change, there was one." When they looked at the modified files, they found a known virus. Well, wait a minute, where did that virus come from?

The CPA firm just built this system from original sources to test out these anti-virus products, so it could only have come from the factory or from one of these defensive products. They checked every floppy disk that had been in contact with this system, and they found a copy of the virus on a write protected original copy of one of the competitor's anti-viral products. That company was not even able to maintain the integrity of their own software distribution for the purpose of a major evaluation, so how can they be trusted to maintain integrity of other peoples' systems?

6.1.5   Beware The Demo Virus

Don't take a demo virus to see how a virus works. There are some companies that will send you demonstration viruses. Their demo disk comes complete with 37 "declawed" viruses. Well, declawed is a relative sort of thing. It turns out one of these declawed viruses was declawed for a standard PC, but not for a Novell network. When somebody installed it on their Novell network, they found out that it spread throughout their network causing damage.

6.1.6   Special Purpose Defenses

Special purpose defenses only make sense under real and present attack. If you have a local university that has the Scores Virus, and if you have MacIntosh computers, and if you have employees going back and forth to that university, it makes a lot of sense to get a Scores Virus defense product in house right away. In fact, it probably makes sense to buy a site license for the university so they can clean up and you don't have to keep worrying about the Scores Virus. But once that attack is gone, it's time to stop using that defense all the time. The reason is, it's just for one specific attack. It takes time and space, and if you did that for every attack, you would have 125 or more different special purpose programs running every time you turned on your computer, checking for these attacks, taking up space, and taking up time. You don't want to end up with thousands of these defenses taking up all your disk space and computer time.

6.2 Product Comparison By Type

There is a hierarchy of defenses available on the market today. The soundest defenses are hardware based with software assistance, while the least sound are pure foolishness. We list them here from most sound to least sound, but please understand that soundness is not the only criterion used in making rational decisions about viral defense.

6.2.1 Hardware Based Protection

The soundest defense is hardware based protection with sound operating system controls. The best kind of protection is a POset, but you can only buy POset structured protection for PCs, where the hardware limits its effectiveness. You can get computers with Bell-LaPadula secrecy, Biba integrity, and compartments, and try to configure it to act like a POset, but this is pretty difficult to do. You can try limited transitivity, but you can't buy any systems that provide it. You should apply limited functionality wherever you can. For example, if you have someone doing data entry, there's no reason for them to have general purpose use of the computer system. It's a perfectly reasonable thing to do.

6.2.2   Integrity Shells

After sound defenses, we have integrity shells. In theory, they're not quite as sound as limited sharing and limited function, but from a practical standpoint, sound protection can only limit viral spread, so integrity shells are probably still a necessary component of a rational defense plan.

6.2.3   Cryptographic Checksums

Cryptographic checksum systems are effective against most common attacks, but they are vulnerable to a number of theoretical and real-world attacks, and they have serious limitations. Furthermore, they are about the same cost as integrity shells, so there is really no good reason to use a cryptographic checksum when you can get a full fledged integrity shell for the same cost.

6.2.4   System Call Detection and Prevention

Some popular defenses try to limit viral spread by intercepting system calls and forcing the user to make protection decisions. These tend to create numerous false positives and false negatives, are very hard for the average user to understand, and only protect against a limited number of attacks. Ultimately, these sorts of systems can be used to simulate hardware based protection. For example, the POset structured PC protection system is based on this technology.

6.2.5 Known Viruses Detectors

Virus scanners and monitors are technologies for searching for known viruses, and are a fairly popular defense, even though they are quite expensive to operate and maintain, and are ineffective against attacks the designer was not aware of at the last distribution. They tend to produce an expensive and false sense of security.

6.2.6 Looking For Questionable Instructions

Some defensive products look through files for known damage routines to try to detect programs that will cause significant harm, but in practice, this defense is ineffective and produces many false positives and false negatives.

6.2.7 Examining Printable Strings

The one ineffective defense that is considered worth using by many people, is a program that searches for printable strings in programs. If the program has a string that says "ha, ha, I got you, I'm deleting all your files", you probably shouldn't run that program. On the other hand, just because a program doesn't state that it deletes all your files, doesn't make it safe to use.

6.3 Opposing Forces

Backing off to the meta level, most organizations have a set of opposing forces that have to be dealt with. Of particular technical interest is the opposition of sharing, secrecy, and integrity.

- We need sharing, otherwise every secretary has to write the operating system from scratch ... "Sorry, I can't give you a disk with the operating system, that would be sharing".

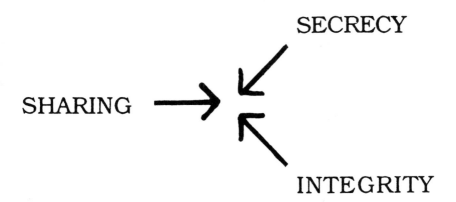

Figure 6.1: Opposing Forces

- Secrecy has a lot of historical momentum, 5,000 years of it. When manufacturers first started making computers, they designed them to maintain secrecy, because the military was the first major user. From the 1940s through the 1960s, the military had a strong influence on these decisions because they drove the market.

- In the mid 1980s, integrity corruption became widespread because of the rampant spread of computer viruses. As a result, a far broader and more critical need for integrity has arisen.

Unfortunately, we cannot have perfect secrecy, perfect integrity, and perfect sharing, all at the same time. We have to decide which we want where. That means we have to find an appropriate mix for our environment, reexamine it periodically, understand and audit for weaknesses, and continue to address the conflict over time.

6.4 Management Tools

Although basic technical safeguards are important, you need adequate management tools to deal with protection at any level. Let me give you some examples of how inadequate our management tools are.

A typical PC has about 10,000 bits of protection information, a typical engineering workstation has about 100,000 bits of protection information, a typical LAN based file server has about 1 million bits of protection information, and a typical mainframe computer system has about 10 million bits of protection information. Right now, the way we manage all those protection bits is one bit at a time!

Well guess what, nobody is able to handle 10 million bits of information properly without good tools. Two surveys were done in 1988 of large MVS shops. One was done by the Office of Management and Budget in the United States, the other one was done by a major CPA firm. The results were reported in the New York DPMA Computer Virus Clinic.

- In industry 80% of the systems, and in the government 90% of the systems, did not adequately use the protection mechanisms in place. In other words, they had protection mechanisms there to use, but they just couldn't manage them. Now, I don't believe that's the fault of the systems administrators. I think it's because they didn't have adequate tools.

At the same conference, there was somebody there from Computer Associates (the company that maintains ACF2, a security packages for MVS), and they said it's no problem to properly manage protection in MVS. All you have to do is properly manage the 15 protection related modules and not make any error in any of those 15 modules and you will be safe from attack. Well, let's see, in a typical MVS shop you might have 100,000 users. With 100,000 users, how often does somebody get hired or fired? One hundred employee changes per working day would mean that 25000 changes per year, or an average employee turnover time of 4 years. How many people shift jobs a day? Oh, probably another 200, that's a promotion or job change every two years. How often do we add or remove access to a given user? You get the idea.

In a typical day in a typical MVS shop, you have 1,000,000 or more bits of protection state changing. That's why a big MVS shop has a lot of people working on protection. In one very efficient MVS shop discussed in a short course, there were 8 people dedicated to protection for 500 users. That's 1.6% of the computing personnel, or 1,600 full time people for a 100,000 user system, and an average of about 1000 bits set per protection person per day, or several protection bit changes per person per minute. That's too much overhead just to set all these bits, especially if they still can't set all the bits right all of the time. What we have to do is devise tools to manage these protection systems, otherwise it's a hopeless case.

6.5   Summary

The most practical technical defenses today are limited sharing, limited function, and integrity shells. It is likely that a combination of these three will dominate integrity protection in computers for a long time to come, and that they will form the basis for effective controls in the future. Some hope still remains for advances in N-version programming and sound change control, particularly in the areas of automated programming and program verification, but these are all very long term possibilities, and they are very computing intensive relative to today's computing environment.

Chapter 7

Non-Technical Defenses

Although technical defenses are central to success against computer viruses in the modern environment, history has shown that no technical method alone is effective for information protection. Any system must be used by people, and people must make decisions about what methods to use and how to use them. We will now discuss how the technical issues in virus defense lead to management decisions, and the basis for making these decisions.

7.1 Reactive And Proactive Defense

One dimension of the defense problem is the proactive versus reactive issue.

7.1.1 Reactive Defenses

Historically, reactive defenses have been widely used in computer security. The problem with reactive defenses is that they depend on people noticing the side effects of an attack without computer assistance, and then correcting the problem with a lot of hard work.

As we have seen, many of the viruses that may come up don't have easily identifiable symptoms, once corruption is detected the source isn't always obvious, and there may be a great deal of effort required to undo the damage once it is detected. Let me give a few examples.

- The Internet Virus was in an environment where, even though substantial security controls were in place in much of the network, the entire network was unusable for several days, because there were no proactive integrity controls in place.

- The mainframe Christmas card attack brought down thousands of mainframes for several hours and left aftershocks for weeks. Again, good computer security controls were in place, but there were no proactive integrity controls.

The major disadvantages of reactive defenses are that they take a lot of time, systems fail during the reaction time of the defense, and they don't anticipate problems that may not be recoverable without prior preparation. The major advantage of reactive defense is that it costs nothing unless an attack takes place (at which time it usually costs a great deal).

7.1.2   Proactive Defenses

Proactive defenses have definite advantages, in that they anticipate the potential for attacks and act to protect against them.

Special purpose proactive defenses have been in place for quite some time, but they tend to be relatively ineffective. For example, there is a product called CA Examine (by Computer Associates) that works on ACF2 based mainframes. It "knows" the operating system, so if somebody writes a virus that gets into the operating system of ACF2, CA Examine may pick it up. The same is true of virus scanners and monitors. Although they are successful against well known attacks, they are completely ineffective against new attacks, attacks without obvious side effects, hard to track viruses, and evolutionary viruses.

General purpose proactive defenses have been in place since 1985, and they are the only automated defenses that have ever "discovered" a new virus. Without these defenses, no subtle virus would likely be discovered, because there would be no behavioral change for users to notice.

7.2 Major Methods Used Today

The major methods in use today are limited sharing, integrity shells, virus scanners, administrative controls, and auditing.

7.2.1 Limited Sharing

Limited sharing is expensive, and doesn't detect viruses. It effectively limits the spread of viruses if it is used properly, but almost no organization uses limited sharing properly. This is the basis by which the U.S. DOD network was (supposedly) separated from the Internet. Unfortunately, these controls were not properly implemented or used, and thus the DOD network was infected through gateways that were supposedly secure. Once the Internet Virus got through, the DOD decided to use better isolation. Unfortunately, this makes it still harder for the newest technologies to be integrated in to DOD systems. This is called the chilling effect.

The second limited sharing strategy is isolation during attack. IBM says when an attack is detected in the network, they "pull the plug". That doesn't mean they are safe. If a virus has been spreading for six months and goes off today, pulling the plug in the network isn't going to help. On the other hand, if the attack is not a slow or subtle one, pulling the plug might help.

So let me ask you, who here knows where the plug is? Do any of you operate a computer network? Do you know where the plug is to disconnect yourself from the rest of the world? Let me tell you IBM did not know where the plug was. When the Christmas card attack took place, they just didn't know how to immediately disconnect from outside networks. Now they know.

In many organizations there isn't one plug, there are 50 of them. If you are going to go to isolation, you have to know how to do it. There has to be somebody that knows where the plug is, and there has to be a contingency plan in place to assure that the plug can be pulled effectively.

One form of limited sharing that is somewhat effective and in widespread use, is the separation of R&D from Production. We pointed out many of the problems and features of this method earlier.

Other common forms of limited sharing include; not permitting external floppy disks or tapes into a facility, requiring all incoming programs to be checked through a central clearing house, and other similar procedural methods. These will be discussed in more depth under a separate heading.

7.2.2   Integrity Shells

Integrity shells are the most cost effective virus defense available today, and are becoming the dominant virus defense technology. They exist for Unix and DOS, and new versions for other systems are under development. They are not free, but they are very cost effective, as we will discuss later.

There are many installations in the mainframe environment and other environments that use cryptographic checksums. They typically build in-house systems that are mediocre relative to the commercial products, but they are reasonably effective once they are put in place. As an example, the Federal Reserve Bank in the United

States uses cryptographic checksums to verify their change controls.

7.2.3   Virus Scanners

Virus scanners seem inexpensive, but update costs, day to day scanning costs, and cleanup costs after attack detection, makes this method quite expensive in actual use (we will discuss this in some depth later). Scanners are also ineffective against new viruses and evolutionary viruses. Perhaps the most difficult issues in the purchase of scanners, is the plethora of known viruses. I am aware of about 500 computer viruses at this time, and none of the scanners on the market (as of this writing) scan for more than about 150 of them. Several vendors claim to scan for "all N known viruses", where N is a number between 27 and 150. It is not hard for a decent programmer to create one new virus every hour or so. Some experts even claim that the number of viruses detected is such a marketing factor that some defense companies generate new viruses just to claim a higher number of viruses detected in their products. Clearly, the likelihood of getting a particular virus should also be a factor in the list of viruses being scanned for.

Despite their many problems, scanners are one of the dominant technologies on the market. In some sense, this demonstrates the ignorance of the computer security community to the real issues in virus defense, but to a greater extent, it reflects the analogy between biological disease and computer viruses. When we are sick, we are used to going to a doctor and getting a test. Once the disease is determined, we hope there is a known cure. Virus scanners are thought of like regular medical checkups. The problem is that we could do a lot better by spending more money on preventative medicine.

The scanning approach tends to lead us away from better solutions that apply to computers but don't yet apply to people. You could think of better virus defenses in the same light as genetic ther-

apy which makes us immune to large classes of diseases. Computers
are a lot simpler than people, and as a result, we have developed
types of genetic therapy that are far more cost effective and reliable
than scanners.

7.2.4 Administrative Controls

Administrative controls tend to be very inexpensive and very ineffective. The problem seems to be that a single error or omission in
the application of a policy can cause widespread collapse. Despite
this problem, the low cost of administrative controls makes them
justifiable as a supplement to technical defenses.

An example of an administrative control is the "No External
Disks" policy. It's a great administrative control, and it should probably be used in many cases, but let me tell you about the AIDS attack of 1989. In this attack, tens of thousands of infected floppy disks
were mailed to people on a computer magazine's mailing list. Most
of those subscribers were in organizations with a "no external disks"
policy in place. Despite the administrative control, there were organizations where hundreds of users put these disks into their computer
systems and got the bug. It cost these organizations several man-
months of effort to get rid of the problem, because the employees
didn't follow the policy.

Let me give you another example. An employee showed up at
one door with a floppy disk. The guard said "Didn't you read the
memo? You can't bring in external disks". The employee responded
"This isn't an external disk, it's an internal disk. I took it home
last night, and I'm bringing it back today." The problem is that the
employee did not understand what the policy meant when it said
"No External Disks". If you are going to use administrative and
procedural controls, you have to educate your employees on what
they mean and why they are in place. Typically we don't do that.

We make a regulation, don't bother to explain it, and they interpret it in their own way, or just ignore it.

Another classic administrative control is the "Changes Should Be Approved" policy. Note the wording. It doesn't say we should use sound change control. It says changes should be approved. There is a person with a rubber stamp that says "Approved", and this person stamps every change that goes by. Maybe in a highly sophisticated organization, once a month, the person says "Not Approved - Resubmit", but the vast majority of the changes are simply approved.

This is ineffective as change control, but it is effective in one sense. If you are the President of the company, you may be personally liable for failing to take prudent action. You now have somebody to fire.

Another common technique is to require all software to go through a central clearinghouse before internal use. This is a sensible policy, if only to assure that new programs interact properly with the existing environment. It is not an effective defense against unknown viruses, but it is a rational place to use scanning technology. Even though it won't pick up new viruses, it will be effective against some known viruses, and it will be very low cost because it is only used at one central site.

Eliminating bulletin board access is inexpensive and fairly common as a procedural defense. Some bulletin boards have a reputation for posting Trojan horses, but for the most part, bulletin boards that provide valuable information are worth subscribing to.

A more common policy is the "no shareware" policy. Let me give you some historical facts. No legitimate distribution of public domain software or shareware has ever contained a virus as far as we can tell, but almost every major manufacturer of software has distributed a virus in a legitimate software distribution. At least one disk manufacturer has distributed disks with preloaded operating systems containing viruses. A PC magazine has distributed several thousand copies of a virus in a distribution to its readers. So if we are going to make a sound decision based on historical fact, we should have a policy to only buy shareware and public domain software if we want to avoid viruses, and to never buy "legitimate" shrink-wrapped software.

There are probably some good reasons that shareware and public domain software has never been infected with viruses. When you get shareware or public domain software the author's name is attached. There is a human being whose name is attached to that software, and therefore they have a very good reason to make sure it's right, because it's their reputation that's at stake. On the other hand, if you work for Microsoft and you put in a virus, nobody will ever know who did it and your name will not be on the copyright anyway. So why should you care if it causes problems? Finally, trying to manage protection in an environment where you one person writing a piece of software, is very easy. Trying to maintain protection in an environment with thousands of programmers is not so easy. The probability of a virus getting into Microsoft is much higher than getting into a small software manufacturer's operation.

7.2.5   Auditing

Auditing has been almost completely ineffective in virus defense, and has been minimally successful in tracking down attackers. The first problem is that the available audit trails don't keep enough information to track the progress of a virus.

Many systems have access control facilities that report attempts to violate the access controls, but a virus doesn't have to do anything that's not authorized, so that sort of tracking is ineffective. It only detects attacks that aren't very well written.

Then, there's post-mortem (i.e. *After You're Dead!*) analysis, which works just great, except that it's too late. You know, call the auditor who comes in and tells you that your computer system is indeed not working, and tries to determine everything that was corrupted in the process. It may be the only way to restore the system to its proper state, but in some cases it takes months to resolve, and it doesn't keep you in business while the repairs are underway.

7.3 Testing Defenses Without Viruses

How do you test a defense without a virus? Defenses do specific things. You might start by asking some questions:

- What is the defense supposed to do? (Very often, what it is supposed to do is apply a technique that we know has major problems.)

- Does it really do that? (Very often, protection products don't really do what they claim to do as well as you would think from listening to the claims.)

- How do they do what they do? (Very often, they are based on a good idea, but they don't use the idea properly.)

- Is what they do adequate for your needs? (Very often, products don't fulfill the needs of the customer, and the customer has to choose the better of two inadequate solutions.)

In other words, you first have to address the issue of what you want to protect from what. You have to start by deciding what's worth protecting in your environment, and then you have to provide appropriate protection. To the extent that the defense does what you want done, it's appropriate.

Let me give you an example. There's a defense that came out in the late 1980s when some viruses were attacking the "COM-MAND.COM" command interpreter on PC's. Lots of authors were

writing articles claiming that viruses were programs that modified
the operating system on PC's, and that therefore we could protect
PCs from viruses by protecting COMMAND.COM from modification. I have a saying, "In computer security, ignorance is not bliss,
it's suicide."

So that's what we had, a lot of people shooting themselves in
the foot. They wrote programs to protect COMMAND.COM from
changes by using a copy to verify that the original is unchanged. Well
guess what? It works if the attacker is changing COMMAND.COM
in some limited ways, -AND- not changing the copy, -AND- if we use
it often enough, -AND- if there are no other side effects, -AND- if it's
cost effective to do this. Well, it's almost certainly not cost effective
to do this, but there are still people that do this check every time
they turn on their computer, and until they get another virus, they
think they are completely safe.

7.4   Peer Network Problems

We have already mentioned that procedural methods tend to fail,
but sometimes, these failures can be quite subtle. One example is the
problem in so called "Peer Networks". A peer network is a computer
network were two "peers" at different physical places in the network
have equivalent access rights. The problem with peer networks is that
by making peers in distributed locations equivalent, you also make
all of the protection mechanisms related to those peers equivalent.
Since the protection "chain" is only as strong as its weakest link, you
distribute every weakness at any location to all of its peers.

Say, for example, that in one location (say Pittsburgh) where
people have access to facility A, a specific set of procedural controls
are strictly enforced (e.g. no floppy disks are allowed in, all incoming software is checked for propriety, no physical access is allowed by

unauthorized personnel, and all personnel are well trained). Meanwhile, in another location (say Melbourne), people also have access to facility *A*, and a different set of procedural controls are strictly enforced (e.g. all software goes through sound change control, all personnel are well trained, only listed vendors are used, and only authorized software is executed by the operating system). Each is a good set of techniques, but they don't match well. For example:

- A virus accidentally brought from another site by a printer maintenance person in Melbourne, can't infect Melbourne computers because they won't run unauthorized software. It can however, move over the network to Pittsburgh where, acting as a peer program from Melbourne, it will be trusted to operate. Once the virus infects programs in Pittsburgh, it can then spread back to Melbourne because it comes in authorized programs.

Note that both Melbourn's policy and Pittsburgh's policy, when acting alone, would have prevented infection from this virus. In Pittsburgh, the physical security would have kept the infected disk out, while in Melbourne, the technical defense would have prevented infection, but in concert, the defenses didn't match. It is the combination of peer equivalence and unmatched policies that results in this vulnerability.

We have seen one recurring incident of this sort in a large US government department. Uniform standards were in place across the organization, but one site had very tight procedural defenses, and the other had more technical defenses. As a result, viruses would enter into one site, and through the network, transmit into an equivalent area in the other site.

The Internet virus and the Christmas card were both effective because they operated in peer networks with very similar problems, and most viruses that operate on a single system operate over peer networks because the networks are designed to make peer operation transparent.

In order for procedural methods to work, especially in peer networks, the methods and procedures must be uniform or properly matched. This in turn presents a problem in that procedures are things that people do. It is very hard to get people in two physically different locations to do the same things because of cultural and personal differences.

7.5 Tracking Down Attackers

I have mentioned that auditing techniques are very poor for tracking down viral attackers. To support my contention, I would like discuss the few successes in tracking down viral attackers with EDP audit techniques.

7.5.1 Tracking Down The Christmas Card Attacker

The Christmas card was first detected when it put an end to processing and network communications for about 500,000 users around the world. Since many of these users had Christmas cards on their screens, and all of the time and space was being taken up in the same activity, the immediate source of the problem was self-evident. The virus was in source form, and was only a few lines long, so it didn't take very long for the administrators to find it, determine what it did, and create a special purpose defense against it.

The Christmas card was soon tracked to an attacker in Germany through the use of EDP Audit, which was certainly a magnificent feat in light of the fact that it involved literally millions of transmissions through a global network. It turns out that the networks where the virus was launched kept track of each file sent over the network by sender, receiver, file name and transmission time. Since the Christmas card did not do any infection, the file name used for transmission was always the same. The organizations involved coordinated the effort through the network after the defense was in place, and found the earliest time of transmission. This was the first copy sent, and identified the user who sent it.

7.5.2 Tracking Down The Internet Attacker

Another example of an auditing success was the Internet attack. In the Internet attack, there were some rather obvious behavioral changes. In particular, 6,000 users could do almost nothing with their computer systems. It took a very long time for users of those 6,000 computers to even login, while 60,000 other users effectively couldn't use the computer network. Various individuals decided that something was going wrong, and one of the first things they did was to look at the process table (a simple way to look at all the active processes under Unix, the operating system being effected).

What they found was thousands of processes on their computers. One of the people that took part in tracking this attack down said "I was really impressed, I didn't know this computer could have that many processes" (or some such thing). Over the next day or so, a wide variety of attempts were made to stop the virus from acting, and eventually some of the defenders found a way to stop it from spreading. They had considerable difficulty in communicating the cure because most of the people involved only knew each other by computer mail addresses, and the network was too overloaded to communicate effectively, but eventually they got the word out. By the end of the second day, the network was operating again, and many of the sites had installed defenses.

They then traced packet quantities over time by looking at network statistics gathered by one of the sites in the network as a matter of course, and found was there were an abnormally high number of packets being sent in two regions of the country. One region was in the area between San Francisco, California and San Diego California within about the first 50 miles from the West coast of the United States. That's an area of about 20,000 square miles (60,000 square kilometers). The other region was on the East Coast of the United States, between New England and Southern New York, as far in from the coast as Philadelphia. That's another 20,000 square miles (60,000 square kilometers).

A large percentage of the population of the United States is in those areas, so what they did was search every computer system that was on this network, 60,000 systems or so, in both of these large areas. Imagine if you will, somebody saying there is a carrier of the Bubonic Plague, and that their are either in the New York area or the Los Angeles area, so we are going to go door to door and search every room in Los Angeles and New York to try and find this person. That's what we are talking about in terms of these searches.

Nobody challenged their constitutional right to search all of these computer systems without a warrant. I guess that means that in the United States, we don't have a reasonable expectation of privacy in our computer systems. They did the massive searches and they found a likely source. In the meanwhile, two graduate students at MIT and two graduate students at Stanford University were 'uncompiling' the binary executable program that was determined to be the cause of this problem. It took each team about two days to create a 'C' program that compiled into the identical binary executable program as the 60Kbyte binary part of the virus (which is quite a feat).

They tracked it down to a particular person, found physical evidence to support their contention, tried him, and found him guilty in Federal Court in the United States. Even though he pled innocent to the criminal charges, he admitted to having written the virus.

7.5.3 The AIDS Disk

The last example of tracking down a viral attacker who didn't put
a name and address in the code of the virus or otherwise advertise
their identity, was the case of the AIDS disk. In this case, computerized audit trails were not involved in the process at all. The
attacker was tracked down after tens of thousands of systems began
having serious problems (assuming we have indeed tracked down the
actual attacker), because the list of recipients was purchased from a
company that kept track of the purchaser.

7.5.4 When A Success Is Not A Success

In some sense these were tremendous auditing successes, but I see
them in another light.

One important point is that out of about 150 viruses in the world,
only 3 that did not list their authors have been tracked down to a
source. Furthermore, none of the other attacks in the environment
today will likely ever be tracked to a source. This is partially because
there are no audit trails provided as a normal part of the operating
system on personal computers, but a far more important aspect of
this issue is that modern computer systems do not log the information
that would be required to trace the progress of a virus. If we included
this sort of audit trail, it would take enormous amounts of time and
space, we would have to find new types of tools to allow us to analyze
the audit trail, and it would not significantly reduce the difficulty of
tracking down an attacker.

A far more important problem, in my opinion, is that in every
case, audit has failed to detect the presence of the attack until the
damage became evident due to massive widespread damage. In other
words, it was behavioral changes in the system identified by users
that caused detection. That's pretty disconcerting to me, because if
we had a virus that spread slowly over a couple of years before doing

massive damage, we would be in real trouble. We might even look
on backup tapes and find that the virus was there as far back as our
backups went. Are we going to clean backup tapes from the last six
years?

7.5.5   Needed Improvements In EDP Audit

In order to be effective, our audits should pick up viruses before
behavioral changes take place, and the tools available to the auditor
until recently were simply inadequate to the task. Change control
is inadequate in most cases. Dependencies are rarely considered in
an EDP audit. In an EDP audit they will almost never tell you
that your mailing list could become corrupted and that might cause
all your bills to go wrong. Those indirect things tend to be the
things that cause big problems on computers. We generally think
of it as subtle little bugs, but they are not really that subtle. If we
kept track of what was going on, we could predict this ramification.
That's why understanding the risk analysis we will discuss later is
very important.

7.6   The Problems With Backups

Backups are often touted as an important aspect of virus defense,
and we certainly agree that without other defenses in place, backups are helpful against most attacks, but they are not without their
problems. As we pointed out earlier, backups are safe harbor for
viruses, and thus they present a major spreading and cleanup problem, but there are several other problems with backups in the current
environment.

7.6.1 They Don't Always Work

One of the major problems is that backups don't assure the propriety of what's backed up. I like telling stories, so let me tell you a story about backups.

AT&T has a set of computers that run the Unix operating system, and when you use these systems to do backups, the backup menu asks what would you like to backup:

```
Backup which file structures?

ALL / /usr /usr2
```

The natural choice is, of course, "ALL", but it turns out that if you chose "ALL", you can't restore from backups. As bizarre as that may seem, all of their maintenance people know this, and know how to get around it. If you are not under an AT&T maintenance contract, this can be very expensive.

Let me give you another example of why backups may not be restorable. There is something called head skew, where the tape head used for backups is off at an angle. When you write the tape on a tape drive with a skewed head and use another tape drive to read the tape back, it doesn't work. I had an experience where a tape drive was realigned and then couldn't restore from backups because the tape head was now aligned differently. To restore the backups, I had to misalign the head, adjusting it while trying to read from the tape until the tape started to read correctly. Then I could restore from the backups, after which I had to realign the tape heads and write the backups again with proper tape alignment.

Another problem is with heat. What happens when you put the backups in the back of your car on a sunny day? Well, it doesn't take very long for your backup tapes to become useless. There are many other such problems with the backup tape technology in widespread use today.

So let me ask you, who here has ever had a problem restoring a backup? About 50% of every audience I talk to has experienced a failed backup. If this is your only safety net, you're not very safe, because we can't be sure that the backup works, much less assure that what we backed up was what we wanted to backup.

7.6.2 They Aren't Kept Long Enough

How long should you keep backups? Well, it's a function of what you are doing.

People in the banking industry say that if they have to go back one day, they will be out of business. In this circumstance, week old backups of transaction data are essentially useless except under the rarest circumstances. The reason is that a typical bank transfers its entire assets in electronic funds transfers (EFTs) about twice a week. The "Federal Reserve Bank" of the United States transfers the entire GNP of the United States every day in EFTs. If you lose one day's transactions, can you go back to yesterday and reasonably expect your system is going to work right? Your entire assets will be wrong. So there's no sense in which you can really ever go backwards in that sort of system without months of EDP audit effort.

For a software manufacturer, the situation is much different. Backup copies are very often used to repair old versions of software, to determine why errors are occurring in a particular application, and to assure that new versions don't introduce new problems.

7.6.3 They Act As Safe Harbor For Viruses

The final problem with backups is that they provide safe harbor for viruses. We discussed this in some detail earlier, but we have not discussed how to resolve the problem.

7.7 Recovery From Viral Attack

So how do you recover from a virus attack? It turns out that if you are prepared, it's rather straight forward. Fighter pilots have a saying that goes: "See it, kill it, and get away quickly." That's how you survive as a fighter pilot, and it's about the same for computer viruses.

7.7.1 See It

If you are going to get rid of a virus, you have to see it. If the virus is in your backup system over a six month period, evolving and changing and dropping off little time bombs all over the place, it's going to be too late by the time everything starts failing. If you can't detect it ahead of time, you simply can't get rid of it in the long run. Detection is critical.

The best method of detection at this time is the proper use of cryptographic checksums in integrity shells. Good change control is also a feasible way to enforce integrity. You can, for example, periodically compare change control logs with actual changes on the system. This can be very expensive because it involves repeated manual reexamination.

7.7.2 Kill It

How do you kill it? If you can see it, you can kill it pretty easily. The simplest thing to do is find all the infected programs and delete them. For example, if you are using cryptographic checksums, you can very easily find everything that has changed, restore them from backups, and the virus is exterminated. The reason this works is that, if you can see the virus right away, and if you have done a good job in verifying the propriety of backups, you know the backups are correct, and you can restore them safely.

Well, okay, so how do I assure the propriety of the backups? I got interested in this problem because I have had backups go bad from various mundane problems, and I am the careful sort. What I do to make sure that I have good backups is to restore from the backups onto another computer, and verify their cryptographic checksums. Restoring on another system assures that the backup worked, that the tape can be restored, and that the subsequent checking operations are independent of the system being backed up. Verifying the change control information provides assurance that the information on the tapes corresponds properly to expectations.

As we discussed earlier, when you try to remove a virus during normal processing, you have a race between the cure and new infections, but if you stop all processing, the virus cannot spread, while the cure can eradicate it. In systems with hardware based protection, you can often do a better job at recovery because you don't always have to stop all processing in order to remove the virus. For example, if we know that the virus is only in a few domains in a POset based system, we can continue processing in areas the virus cannot reach with a high degree of assurance that the virus will not spread even though other processing is ongoing.

7.7.3 Get Away Quickly

Each organization has to make its own decisions about prioritizing which of these things to do first and how quickly to do them, but as a rule, each of them should be done. I prioritize them as follows most of the time, but there are exceptions.

1. Isolate the infected systems to prevent further spread.

2. Get copies of the attack code, and send it off to an expert for analysis. If you have a good defense product and it picks up something that nobody has ever see before, the copy will help find any side effects that may have to be corrected. If you have a poor product, it is unlikely to come up with anything new, but you should probably try to get a copy just to be certain.

3. Search out and destroy the virus on your backup media, floppy disks, tapes, and other related systems.

4. Get the system back up and working. You do that by killing all of the copies of the virus, restoring from backups, and restarting user operations.

If you have good detection in place, you don't usually have to do all of these steps because you pick up attacks before they can spread.

7.8 CERT Teams

CERT (Computer Emergency Response Team) teams are groups with responsibility for preparing an organization for emergency response to computer problems, typically including viruses. The CERT team is typically responsible for educating the organization in the area of viruses, training individuals for the actions they will be required to take, determining appropriate technical precautions, and assuring that human and technical systems operate properly. When an actual emergency takes place, these teams usually coordinate the defensive effort.

In the current environment, good CERT teams are almost entirely pro-active in their role. This is because there are sufficient technical defenses to make response to the vast majority of attacks completely automatic. The well prepared CERT team spends its time evaluating protection improvements, educating employees, preparing for disaster recovery, and assuring that policy is aligned to needs.

Less well prepared CERT teams end up in a very different circumstance. They spend anywhere from hours to months cleaning up after attacks, they have to deal with rampant reinfection, and they sometimes have to reenter massive amounts of data from original copies. In one case, a company had to reenter 3 years worth of data because their employees weren't properly educated in how to respond to an attack. They put in backup disk after backup disk in an attempt to recover, only to find that the virus destroyed their backups because they were not write protected. A well prepared CERT team would have prudent methods in place to prevent this problem.

7.9   Conclusions

Remember that protection is an activity, not a product. Any defense will have to start with people making decisions about how to react to corruptions in the environment. To the extent that automated tools help in this decision making process, they are available, but no automated system can take the responsibility away from the people who use it.

Chapter 8

Exposure Analysis

Risk analysis has changed in two basic ways since the advent of computer viruses. The first change is that integrity corruption is now being considered. The second change is that we now have to consider transitive information flow in our analysis. There are also several historical assumptions about defenses that have now become outdated. For example, backups alone don't substantially reduce the risk from computer viruses.

Unfortunately, standard risk analysis makes the assumption that we can associate probabilities with events. Since we don't have any significant amount of reliable data on the factors that contribute to viral attack, it's hard to assess probabilities. Since inadequate detection is the norm, we cannot hope to get significant amounts of reliable data in the near future.

One alternative to risk analysis in this case is exposure analysis. Exposures are essentially the worst case possibilities for loss under a given scenario. We can 'cover' exposures by using appropriate defensive techniques, decide how many simultaneous failures of coverage to tolerate before coverage breaks down, and provide appropriate redundancy to reach that goal.

8.1   The Information Flow Model

I will start the discussion by showing a "subject/object" matrix commonly used to represent access control in modern computer systems.

	DB1	FILE1	BUP	FILE2	FILE3	DB2
Joe	*rw*	*r*			*r*	*r*
Alice		*rw*	*rw*			*r*
Bob			*r*	*rw*		*rw*
Lam		*r*	*w*	*w*	*rw*	

In this model, there are sets of subjects (i.e. Joe, Alice, Bob, and Lam), objects (i.e. DB1, FILE1, BUP, FILE2, FILE3, and DB2), and a set of access 'rights' (i.e. *r*ead, and *w*rite). The matrix is suppose to describe what's allowed and not allowed, but as we will now see, it doesn't quite do that.

Our subject/object matrix says, for example, that Joe can *r*ead or *w*rite DB1. If Joe can *w*rite DB1 and Joe can *r*ead DB1, Joe can *f*low information to himself. I'm going to put that result in a different picture that describes how information flows in a system. This picture is called an information flow matrix, and it is used to describe the flow of information.

	Joe	Alice	Bob	Lam
Joe	*f*			
Alice	*f*	*f*	*f*	*f*
Bob	*f*	*f*	*f*	*F*
Lam	*f*	*f*	*f*	*f*

In this matrix, instead of dealing with 'subjects' and 'objects' and 'rights' of subjects over objects, we deal with information 'domains' and the flow of information between them. Joe can '*f*low' information to Joe, so we put an *f* at the intersection of Joe and Joe in the flow matrix. Let's look at Alice. Alice can *w*rite something that Alice can *r*ead, so Alice can *f*low information to Alice. Alice can *w*rite something that Joe can *r*ead, so Alice can *f*low information to Joe. Alice can also *f*low information to Bob and Lam.

Instead of using these sentences, we can abbreviate the wording by writing equations like this; Bob *f* Joe will mean 'Bob can *f*low information to Joe'; Bob *w* Joe will mean 'Bob can *w*rite something that Joe can *r*ead'; and Bob *r* Joe will mean 'Bob can *r*ead something that Joe can *w*rite'. Let's try it.

Bob *w* Joe $\Rightarrow$ Bob *f* Joe
Bob *w* Alice $\Rightarrow$ Bob *f* Alice
Bob *w* Bob $\Rightarrow$ Bob *f* Bob
Bob *f* Alice AND Alice *f* Lam $\Rightarrow$ Bob *f* Lam

That last one is a bit tricky; Bob can *w*rite information that Alice can *r*ead, and Alice can *w*rite information that Lam can *r*ead, so Bob can *w*rite information that Lam can *r*ead indirectly via Alice. This shows the 'transitivity' property of information flow that was not widely recognized until viruses demonstrated it so clearly by spreading from user to user. In the flow matrix, we use F to differentiate indirect flow as an aide to the reader. Let's press on.

Lam *w* Joe $\Rightarrow$ Lam *f* Joe
Lam *w* Alice $\Rightarrow$ Lam *f* Alice
Lam *w* Bob $\Rightarrow$ Lam *f* Bob
Lam *w* Lam $\Rightarrow$ Lam *f* Lam

So what's the real situation? Everybody except Joe can send information to everybody else. Joe can only send information to himself. If you look at the access matrix, you might think that Alice can not read or write F2, but it's not true. So what this access matrix seems to mean, isn't what it really means at all.

Let's look at another example. I'm going to use the $f$low description from now on, because it's a lot easier than 'read's and 'write's. We have here another flow matrix with a few flows marked, and we are now going to determine all of the flows implied by this matrix. Here we go:

	a	b	c	d	e	f	g	h
a	f	–	–	–	f	f	–	f
b	f	f	–	–	–	–	f	–
c	–	f	f	–	–	–	f	–
d	f	–	f	f	–	–	–	–
e	f	–	–	–	f	–	–	–
f	–	–	–	f	–	f	–	f
g	f	f	–	–	–	f	f	–
h	f	f	f	–	–	–	–	f

$a\ f\ a$ (Given)
$a\ f\ e$ (Given)
$a\ f\ f$ (Given)
$a\ f\ h$ (Given)
$a\ f\ h$ and $h\ f\ b \Rightarrow a\ f\ b$
$a\ f\ h$ and $h\ f\ c \Rightarrow a\ f\ c$
$a\ f\ f$ and $f\ f\ d \Rightarrow a\ f\ d$
$a\ f\ b$ and $b\ f\ g \Rightarrow a\ f\ g$
$a\ f$ Everyone!

So a can flow information everywhere in the system! This was certainly not clear from the initial picture. Let's see what else we can see.

$a \; f \; a$ (Given)
$b \; f \; a$ (Given)
$d \; f \; a$ (Given)
$e \; f \; a$ (Given)
$g \; f \; a$ (Given)
$f \; f \; d$ and $d \; f \; a \Rightarrow f \; f \; a$
$c \; f \; b$ and $b \; f \; a \Rightarrow c \; f \; a$
Everyone $f \; a$!

So now we know that everyone can send information to a. Well, if everyone can send information to a and a can send information to everyone, everyone can send information to everyone else!! This then is the real picture:

	a	b	c	d	e	f	g	h
a	f	f	f	f	f	f	f	f
b	f	f	f	f	f	f	f	f
c	f	f	f	f	f	f	f	f
d	f	f	f	f	f	f	f	f
e	f	f	f	f	f	f	f	f
f	f	f	f	f	f	f	f	f
g	f	f	f	f	f	f	f	f
h	f	f	f	f	f	f	f	f

The chances are, whatever system you have today, this is the case. You have 'read' and 'write' access controls over information, but if you really look at what they imply, chances are that everyone can send information to everyone else. Anyone in your system could damage or leak any and all information.

Let me just point something out for the more mathematically minded among you. If you have a POset, you have an upper triangular matrix. All POsets can be written as upper triangular matrices, and all upper triangular matrices can describe POsets (although they don't necessarily describe all of the implied flows).

Suppose we are concerned about what happens if two people collude to corrupt or leak information. For example, we might like to assure that no three people in our organization can collude to corrupt more than twenty percent of the organization's information. It turns out, that to determine the corruptive effects of collusion, you simply OR the rows of the matrix, and to determine the leakage effects of collusion, you simply OR the columns.

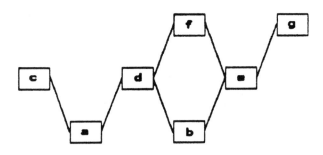

Figure 8.1: Another POset

	a	b	c	d	e	f	g
a	f	–	f	f	–	f	–
b	–	f	–	f	f	f	f
c	–	–	f	–	–	–	–
d	–	–	–	f	–	f	–
e	–	–	–	–	f	f	f
f	–	–	–	–	–	f	–
g	–	–	–	–	–	–	f

In this example, if a and b collude to corrupt information, they can corrupt the OR of their rows in the matrix. Let's look at it. If a launches a virus, it could potentially get to a, c, d and f, while if b launches a virus, it get to b, d, e, f, and g. Between a and b, everything is corruptible.

	a	b	c	d	e	f	g
a	f	–	f	f	–	f	–
b	–	f	–	f	f	f	f
=	f	f	f	f	f	f	f

Corruptions

Similarly if you are worried about leaking secrets, c, d, and g could collude to leak information from everywhere except f.

	c	d	g	$=$
a	f	f	$-$	f
b	$-$	f	f	f
c	f	$-$	$-$	f
d	$-$	f	$-$	f
e	$-$	$-$	f	f
f	$-$	$-$	$-$	$-$
g	$-$	$-$	f	f

Leakage

This gives us an efficient and easy to use way of automatically analyzing systems for the affects of collusion.

The technique is quite simple. First, we have to take transitivity into account by finding all of the indirect information flows and putting them in the matrix. In this example, we have already done this part of the process, which is why we call it a "flow control matrix" rather than a "flow matrix". To determine the effect of collusion on leakage, we 'OR' the columns of the colluding domains in the flow control matrix. To determine the effect of collusion on corruption, we 'OR' the rows of the colluding domains in the flow control matrix.

8.2   The New Exposure Analysis

Now that we understand how systems can be modeled and analyzed using information flows, exposure analysis becomes straight forward. We will use the following POset as our an example to demonstrate the analysis.

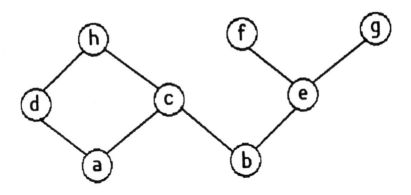

Figure 8.2: A POset

	a	b	c	d	e	f	g	h
a								
b								
c								
d								
e								
f								
g								
h								

The first step in the analysis is to convert the POset into a flow control matrix describing its behavior. Although this will not be necessary to analyze our small example, you will find it most useful for more complex systems. Begin by putting in the flows shown directly in the picture, and then add the indirect flows. When you're done, you should have a picture with 20 *f* marks in it.

The next step is to analyze the effects of corruption and leakage in your organization. This involves considerable effort, but if you have done risk analysis before, most of the information should already be available. If not, you should probably consider it as an important step toward understanding your exposures. We have provided a set of "local" leakage and corruption exposures for this example, and have started to fill out the table with results. You should fill out the rest of the table once you understand how to perform the analysis.

	(local) leakage	(local) corrupt	(global) leakage	(global) corrupt
a	25	75	25	360
b	250	10	250	1335
c	1000	25		
d	750	250	775	260
e	90	200		
f	75	90		
g	25	1000		
h	10	10	2035	10

Every domain has local corruption and leakage values. The "local" corruption value is the total financial damage resulting from the worst case corruption of information in that domain alone. For example, if we have a mailing list with names, addresses, and postal codes, the worst case corruption in this domain alone would be the amount of money required to replace, repair, or reenter the mailing list. In this case, we have assessed 10 billion dollars (all numbers here are in billions of dollars). We have a 10 unit local corruption value associated with that mailing list, because we can re-enter it very easily.

Even though correcting any corruption in this domain may be

quite inexpensive, the effect of the domain becoming corrupted might be horrendous. For example, suppose you are sending out bills using the corrupt mailing list. Your use of the corrupt information may cause you to miss payments for a month or more, generate automatic collection letters, and otherwise damage your business and customer relations. Those are indirect effects of a corruption. Since a virus can spread anywhere information can go, we have to consider the corruption value of every reachable domain as part of the global effect of corruption. The result is that a corruption in b could effect b, c, e, f, g, and h (the columns with f marked in b's row of the flow control matrix). In order to get the global corruption value of b, we add up the local corruption values of these domains and place the sum in the table. I urge you to do this for all of the remaining entries as practice. Is there a mistake in the way I filled out an entry?

The analysis for leakage is essentially the same, except that we look at columns instead of rows in the flow control matrix, and we add local leakage values instead of corruption values to get the total exposure. The "local leakage" value is the worst case damage that could result from all the information in that domain being leaked in the worst possible way (i.e. the Murphy's Law leakage). To determine the global leakage exposure of h, we look at column h in the flow control matrix (once it is filled out), and determine that we have to add up the leakage values of a, b, c, d, and h. Again, I urge you to fill out the remainder of the table and determine whether I have made any mistakes.

8.3 A Cost Analysis Of Virus Defenses

Exposure analysis is one part of the picture, but on the other side of the coin, we have to analyze the costs of defenses in order to determine the most cost effective way to cover exposures. The major competing technologies for viral defense in the market today are virus scanners, virus monitors (programs that scan for known viruses just before execution), cryptographic checksums, and integrity shells, so we will limit our discussion to these cases.

We will avoid undue description here by starting out with formulas that describe the total costs per year of attack and defense. The interested reader can locate more detailed information through the annotated bibliography. We begin by defining terms:

T_s	Total for scanner	s	systems
T_c	Total for crypto checksum	c	checks/year
T_m	Total for monitor	e	employee cost/min
T_i	Total for integrity shell	u	dist-cost*update-count
t_s	minutes per scan	t_c	minutes per check
l_s	license for scanner	l_c	license crypto-checksum
l_m	license for monitor	l_i	license integrity shell
a_n	new attacks	a_o	old attacks
r_s	system cleanup costs	r_f	file cleanup costs
d	distribution costs	o_i	comm-rate[K/c]

Most of these terms are self explanatory, but a few are a bit obscure. The licensing cost for crypto-checksums and integrity shells is normally a one-time cost, whereas for scanners and monitors, regular updates force licenses to be paid over time. To compensate, we use 10% per year of the total licensing cost for integrity shells and crypto-checksums as an equivalent to the yearly licensing cost for scanners and monitors. o_i is a term that describes the rate of spread of a virus, and has experientially been about 2 for a typical PC in a typical environment, and about 10 for a typical PC in a LAN environment.

Now we show the equations for total cost:

$$T_s = s[cet_s + l_s + u] + a_n r_s s + a_o r_s o_i + d$$

$$T_c = s[(cet_c) + l_c] + [a_n + a_o]r_s o_i + d$$

$$T_m = s[l_m + u] + a_n r_s s + a_o r_f + d$$

$$T_i = sl_i + [a_n + a_o]r_f + d$$

Since d, the cost of initial distribution, appears in all equations, we can eliminate it for purposes of comparisson without loss of information.

To make comparissons, it is easiest to subtract equations. We begin by comparing T_s to T_c as follows:

$$T_s - T_c = s[ce[t_s - t_c] + [l_s - l_c + u]] + a_n r_s [s - o_i]$$

Unless checking is so rare that all systems get infected before checking detects an infection, $o_i << s$, which leads to:

$$ce[t_s - t_c] + u + [l_s - l_c] + a_n r_s$$

With daily scanning or checking, any reasonable difference in licensing fees are dominated by scanning and checking costs. Update costs also tend to dominate licensing fee differences for this sort of system, so we can simplify in most cases to:

$$u - ce(t_c - t_s) + a_n r_s$$

so scanners are less expensive if and only if:

$$u + a_n r_s > ce(t_c - t_s)$$

In other words, if update and recovery costs from new attacks combine to exceed the cost difference between scanner scanning times and checksum checksumming times, scanners are less expensive than cryptographic checksums. Using typical values, we compute \$750/year in checking cost difference between the two systems. Thus, if recovery costs are kept low, scanning times don't increase significantly, and relatively few new viruses enter the environment each year, then scanning for known viruses is more cost effective than periodically looking for changes with cryptographic checksums.

We now compare scanners to monitors:

$$T_s - T_m = scet_s + (l_s - l_m) + a_o[r_s o_i - r_f]$$

We assume that licensing fees for scanners and monitors are approximately the same relative to scanning costs. We also note that $o_i > 1$ for any reasonable scenario, and the cost to clean a system (r_s) is normally far greater than the cost to clean a single file (r_f). We then get:

$$T_s - T_m = scet_s + a_o r_s$$

Since all of the terms are positive, T_s is always greater than T_m, and thus periodic scanning for known viruses always costs more than monitoring for known viruses in each program just before it is run.

Now the costs of checksums and integrity shells:

$$T_c - T_i = s[(l_c - l_i) + cet_c] + [a_n + a_o](r_s o_i - r_f)$$

Assuming that licensing costs are not large relative to periodic checksumming costs, we can drop the $(l_c - l_i)$ term. Since $o_i > 1$ for any reasonable system, and system repair costs are almost always more expensive than repair of a single file, we simplify to:

$$T_c - T_i = scet_c + [a_n + a_o]r_s o_i$$

Since all of these terms are positive, T_c is always greater than T_i, and thus checking each program for change just before running it is always more cost effective than periodic system-wide change detection with cryptographic checksums.

Finally, we will compare integrity shells to monitors:

$$T_m - T_i = s[(l_m - l_i) + u] + a_n r_s s + a_o r_f - [a_n + a_o] r_f$$

$$= s[(l_m - l_i) + u] + a_n[r_s s - r_f]$$

The number of systems s is always at least 1, and for any reasonable system, $r_s >> r_f$. If we assume that yearly licensing cost differences are small compared to update costs, we get a per system cost difference of:

$$T_m - T_i = u + a_n r_s$$

We conclude that integrity shells are always less expensive than virus monitors because all of these terms are positive. The cost difference comes from the update cost required to keep monitors up to date, and the cost of cleanup for attacks that monitors don't detect.

Another way to look at this result is that in order for a monitor to be more cost effective than an integrity shell, the yearly licensing cost of an integrity shell must exceed the yearly licensing cost of a monitor by the update cost and the undetected attack cleanup cost.

For monitors to be more cost effective than integrity shells in a case where updates cost \$5 per system and are done each quarter, and assuming no unmonitored attacks happen, integrity shell license costs would have to exceed monitor license costs by \$200 per system! This is because the yearly update cost comes to \$20 per system for monitors, and there is no update cost associated with integrity shells. The $20 per year monitor cost is approximately equivalent to borrowing $200 per system for excess licensing fees of an integrity shell. Integrity shells on the market today cost under $100 per system in moderate quantities, and are thus always more cost effective than any of these other techniques.

It also turns out that as system performance increases, integrity shells and crypto-checksums become less expensive faster than scanners and monitors. This is because improved performance makes checksumming faster and disk improvements make on-line backups cheaper, while the update costs of monitors and scanners stay the same, and the number of viruses that have to be checked goes up.

On-line backups turn out to have negligible costs relative to other options for repair, and their costs decrease with time and the evolution of computers. For example, current disk prices are on the order of $10/Mbyte, while the average system has relatively little information suitable for on-line backup, and for a small reduction in performance, file compression can reduce on-line backups costs even further.

Except under the most contrived circumstances, integrity shells are the most cost effective of the anti-virus techniques currently available for untrusted systems, and this gap will widen with the passage of time.

8.4   Summary

This has been a very mathematical chapter compared to the rest of the book, so it calls for a very non-mathematical summary. Here it is:

- The main change in exposure comes from the fact that viruses spread from program to program, from user to user, from system to system, and from network to network.

- Current systems tend to hide risks rather than clarify them.

- The most cost effective virus defense in almost all situations is the integrity shell.

Chapter 9

Some Typical Scenarios

In almost any scenario you can name, classical defenses will fail miserably, and massive losses of time and data will result. We will go through a few examples to clarify the situation.

9.1 Typical Attacks

- The manufacturer of your most recent software acquisition had a virus and didn't know it. You installed the new software, and the virus spread throughout your computers for a few weeks before damage began to occur. You didn't notice the damage at first because it was widely scattered and only a few problems were reported, but by now you are having thousands of files damaged every day and your operations are failing on a widespread basis. Your backups are infected and you don't know where the virus came from or how far back you have to go to get a clean backup.

- A user brought a floppy disk home to do some late night work, and the disk got infected by a PC product at home. After about three weeks, the virus spread throughout your firm's PCs and now it is starting to wreak havoc ...

- A systems programmer thought he was about to be fired, so he introduced a virus into a library program, and then removed the infection from the source code. As other users used the libraries, other libraries and user files became infected. The attacker then recompiled the library with the clean source before the next backup, to remove the last trace of the cause. After about three weeks, the infected executables slowly migrated to the production system, and ...

- A rival firm sent a spy to sabotage your facility. The spy got a job as a computer operator on the graveyard shift, and began introducing viruses into your system at the rate of about one a day over a three month period. All of the viruses had long delays between infection and damage, large use based delays, or delays based on conditions that are likely to come up only once a year or so. Each was designed to cause random changes in data files, occasional systems crashes, periodic slowdowns, or other minor mischief. By the time the first one was discovered, there were hundreds of viruses of different designs and evolutionary capabilities throughout all of the systems in the company. The delay was so long, that even the six months of backups you maintain contained multiple infections ...

Most of the people that look at these scenarios believe that they are vulnerable to some or all of these attacks. At this point, I usually ask: "So what are you going to do?" After all, it's almost the end of the course, and you believe that your systems are vulnerable to a wide range of devastating attacks. Tomorrow morning, you will be back in your organization, and I want to know what you are going to do about it. To do nothing in light of what we now know would

be negligent at best, so that is not an acceptable answer . . . I'll wait
. . .

$$\vdots$$

To help answer the "What are you going to do?" question, I have devised a series of problems that are designed to demonstrate a wide variety of situations that are likely to be encountered in the current computing environment.

9.2   The Small Business Scenario

You own a small business with 5 physically secure timeshared unix computers, networked with limited functionality (for data transfers and database updates only). With the exception of your programmer, who you trust implicitly (because he's your brother and he owns 1/2 the business), all of the users use the system only through a menu system that does not allow any programming whatsoever. Should you be worried? About viruses? About your brother? Should you buy a viral defense product? How much should you spend?

The first question that usually comes up is whether you should trust your brother, but it turns out this is irrelevant to the virus issue because he's the systems programmer, and can do whatever he wants. He doesn't need a virus to do it.

The limited functionality of the system makes viral attack by the user community essentially impossible if it is properly implemented, but unfortunately, almost nobody does this properly. Let's assume that it is done right for the purposes of this example.

The last possibility is that he might accidentally import some infected software. We almost all depend on some external software from time to time, and if that contains a virus, then the virus may spread throughout the system. That's probably the biggest exposure in this environment.

Now that we know the exposure of concern, let's quickly review the possible defenses. For perfect defense, we can limit sharing, limit transitivity, or limit functionality. We have limited function as far as possible, but we cannot do that effectively for imported software. We cannot limit transitivity in practice today. Unix allows us to limit sharing, and to the extent that this is appropriate, we should use the Unix group facility to prohibit interaction with external software wherever possible.

In the way of imperfect defenses, we have change control, multi-version programming, and integrity shells. Change control doesn't really apply to external software since we cannot normally get sources or effectively deal with changes using limited personnel. Multi-version programming is too expensive for this application. Only integrity shells are left, and they can be used inexpensively and transparently in this environment.

So there we have it, you should combine limited sharing with integrity shells to defend against the external virus threat in this environment, and continue to use limited function against the internal threat.

9.3   The University Scenario

You are the president of a major university with a $100,000,000 research budget, thousands of computers of all sorts, networks running everywhere, 40,000 students who take computer courses, and no defenses against viruses in place. You were infected by the Internet virus in 1988, and five other viruses have shown up on campus since. The student newspaper is pressing the issue, the faculty is protesting the heavy handed way you treat these attacks, and your budget for computers is running low. Should you be worried? About viruses? Should you buy a virus defense product?   How much should you spend?

Let's try to be systematic again this time. We'll start with exposures, then go through the feasible defenses and see how they apply. Let's begin by listing the sorts of systems we are likely to encounter in a university. We will have a financial system, an inventory control system, a system for keeping track of academic records, etc. These are usually grouped under the heading of administrative systems. In a university, we usually also have a large assortment of computers used for educational and research purposes, typically called academic systems. In addition to the computers, there are normally a wide range of networks and gateways to provide connectivity both within the campus and with external networks like the Internet and the EDUnet. In most cases, this network includes the university telephone system.

We have three major exposures to consider; administrative systems, academic systems, and networking systems. To the extent that they interact, we also have to consider the interactions. Each system typically has different vulnerabilities because of its use and users. If all of these systems interact arbitrarily with each other, the whole environment will act as one homogeneous network, and all of the threats in each environment will be threats to the entire environment. Let's start from there and wee what we can come up with.

We only have 5 possibilities worth considering; limited sharing, limited function, sound change control, multi-version programming, and integrity shells.

Can we limited sharing in the university environment? Certainly. For example, the administrative systems do not have to be connected to the educational systems, and the academic systems do not always have to be connected to the research systems. The separation of administrative systems is straight forward, but separating research systems from educational systems is not usually feasible because there is a common community and the sorts of controls used in industry simply would not be tolerated in a university environment.

In the administrative system, we can further limit sharing by separating the grades from the financials, etc., and we should do so wherever appropriate. In this system, we can also limit function for the vast majority of users. For example, a data entry clerk putting grades into the computer need not be able to write programs in the administrative system. Next, we can use sound change control. In this sort of system, change control is often feasible because there are relatively few changes, and they are made by a small number of people. Unfortunately, we still cannot control the incoming vendor software or maintenance people, so we should really augment this with an integrity shell. Finally, multi-version programming is again too expensive.

In the academic computing environment, things are quite different. Limited sharing is generally considered a hindrance to the communications necessary in order to have effective learning. On the other hand, when most academics are questioned, they feel that some things should be protected and others should not. Nevertheless, limited sharing is widely frowned upon. Limited function is also infeasible in most areas of academic computing because most of the software is in support of research, and therefore must be changeable. Sound change control and multiversion programming are also inappropriate to the academic experimental environment. The only alternative is an integrity shell approach.

9.4   The Financial Institution Scenario

You are the computer security chief at a major financial institution. You use ACF2 on your mainframes, a Novell network for your PCs, and have an institutional policy against importing software. You have a corporate programming staff of 2,000, and feel you are in good control over changes in source code. Your production machine is well separated from non-critical machines, you use a limited functionality cryptographically covered network for EFTs, you do background checks on all of your employees, and each is bonded up to $1,000,000. You are insured with $100,000,000 deductible for EFT theft, and you have independent EDP audits performed quarterly. Your boss (the CEO) says the board wants a report in one month on what you have done to protect from viral attack and what you are planning in the way of future defenses. Come up with one.

By now, the technique should be getting automatic. We begin with the exposures, and then look at techniques for coverage. In this scenario however, the analysis has some special features. In particular, electronic funds transfer requires special consideration because the exposure is so high. A typical bank transfers its entire assets in EFTs several times per week. Let's consider that first.

An EFT is really quite a simple transaction. It normally consists of a source account identifier, a recipient account identifier, an amount of money, and an authentication string. That means that limited function applies. Similarly, EFTs can easily be controlled from a single physically secure site and not connected to other computers except through limited function interfaces which carry transactions. Thus, we can have complete isolation except for these limited function links. Because the operations performed are quite simple, there should be very few changes required to the software, so sound change control can also be used here. Similarly, because of the enormous exposure and simple, well specified nature of the interactions, we can sometimes even afford multiversion programs and redundant hardware to support it. Finally, we can use integrity shells to provide independent verification by multiple parties. In other words, this is one application where we can apply all of our techniques.

In some sense, my report to the CEO would begin and end there. I would explain that the exposure from EFT fraud or corruption is so enormous that we have concentrated our efforts there. I would list those techniques already in place and provide a plan for implementing the remainder of the techniques over time.

On the other hand, there are some other problems to address in the remainder of the environment, and I would be remiss if I didn't discuss them.

You have 2,000 programmers and you claim you are in good control over changes. Who believes that? I do not. I don't believe that you can be in good control over changes for more than a couple of programmers. I am sure some people do believe that it's possible, and maybe it is, but it's just very hard for me to believe that 2,000 programmers can be well controlled. For one thing, that would mean another 4,000 programmers doing change control, and I don't know of any company willing to spend that much money without a sound financial basis.

The other problems I see are with the Novell network and institutional policy against importing software. As we have discussed, these are ineffective against viruses, and if the exposures in these areas justify defense, some technical measures should be taken. Since limited function and limited sharing are not feasible in this type of arrangement at this time, and multiversion programming and change control are so expensive relative to the risk, I would almost certainly implement an integrity shell in a mode that prevented the introduction of new software without explicit authorization. This would satisfy both the corporate policy and the legitimate need for coverage in the Novell network.

In my report to the CEO, I would include these facts and provide a plan (along with a funding request) to implement these techniques.

9.5   The Computer Company Scenario

You work for AT+T information services as the chief of corporate computer security for product lines. You deliver general purpose systems to hundreds of thousands of companies and are charged with assuring that their systems operate appropriately. You deliver cryptographic telephones to the US government for communicating classified information. You have an installed base of 500,000 computers that get software upgrades once each year. You have 10,000 programmers working for you, and about one a week is called on the carpet for 'security' violations. This virus thing caught you by surprise, and the CEO is about to tear your head off because last week, the entire internal network went down for 2 days, and the best you could do was keep the word from getting out that you were hit too. Besides buying stock in Maalox, what should you do?

At this point, (having heard the good joke *(see the appendix)* a few hours earlier), someone usually suggests "Prepare three envelopes".

Let's get systematic yet again, only this time, I'll ask the questions, and I want you to come up with the answers.

- What are the exposures?

- Can I limit sharing? How and where?

- Can I limit function? How and where?

- Does sound change control apply? Where? When?

- Does multiversion programming apply? Where? When?

- Do integrity shells have a place? Where? When?

9.6   The Immediate Issue Scenario

You just attended a short course on computer viruses, and got free floppy disks with some sample defense products. What precautions are you going to take with this disk?

Chapter 10

Finishing Up

Before finishing this short course, I would like to take this opportunity to mention a few things I would like you to do. First and foremost, I think you should read the appendices to this book. They include "The Good Joke" that I tell after lunch at my short courses, and a description of some of the technical papers in the field.

The good joke is one of the best computer security related jokes I know of, and I tell it in almost every short course I give as a way to wake people up after the lunch break. Although I am pretty funny sometimes, I did not think of this joke, so I won't claim credit for it. On the other hand, I have embellished it greatly over the years, so even if you have heard it, you might review it to keep up to date.

We have spent a great deal of time and effort discussing the negative impact of computer viruses, but we should also pause to consider that viruses have a great deal of potential for producing positive changes in the computing environment. The mathematical model of viruses shows that any result that can be computed by a computer can be evolved by a virus. When combined with their ability to replicate and spread in networks, this makes viruses a viable option for programming in parallel processing environments. Viruses in limited function environments have already shown great promise. Some researchers have already found that simple to implement viral programs perform nearly as well as optimal parallel processing algorithms in some applications. Other viruses are being used as components in distributed simulation engines.

10.1   Organizational Effects

In light of the advent of computer viruses, many organizations are making major adjustments to their longstanding information protection policies, while other organizations are creating protection policies for the first time because they finally have an identifiable threat that has caused real damage. Many organizations have recently gone through a complete reassessment of their previous protection policies.

In nearly all cases, virus protection is severely lacking today, and although this situation is changing rapidly, there is a large window of vulnerability.

Even in organizations that have implemented internal controls, there is a major vulnerability due to the dependency on external vendors. As we have discussed, many major software vendors have shipped infected programs, and almost every substantial organization using computers today depends on these vendors for their software.

Integrity concerns are growing dramatically, while secrecy concerns are becoming less dominant in the vast majority of applications. This becomes especially important in light of the tradeoff between secrecy, integrity, and sharing.

There has also been a dramatic shift in the perception and role of computer security people. They used to be perceived as the people that made you change your password all the time and kept getting in the way of useful work, but with the increasingly dramatic and damaging integrity corruption due to viruses, this perception is changing.

People in information protection are now perceived as the people in charge of making sure the right information gets to the right place at the right time.

This is just part and parcel of the shift towards a holistic view of the protection function. Protection is now being considered more and more in the design phase instead of as an afterthought.

10.2 User Effects

Along with organizational changes come user changes. In the short run we have seen some severe inconveniences due to inadequate protection, lost privileges as protection policy is tightened, and performance changes as protection mechanisms are put into place. This process is often done insensitively, and thus creates numerous personnel problems that could be avoided by more prudent action. The key to success in implementing these changes seems to be informing the users of what is happening and why it is happening.

In the long run, protection will become more transparent, more thoroughly integrated into the computing environment, and more reliable. We are already seeing improvements in system design to compensate for the virus threat, and if history repeats itself, we will see hardware mechanisms based on the principles outlined here within the next few years. This trend toward higher integrity computer systems will likely have dramatic and long lasting effects on the computing environment.

10.3 What To Expect

The impact of viruses has already been felt throughout the world, and there is no indication that it will be reduced in the near future. In fact, all indications are that the number of new viruses will continue to increase, that the number of incidents with viruses will continue to increase, and that viruses will become more and more embedded in the computing environment. Viruses are already a global problem, with reports of incidents coming in regularly from almost every nation on Earth. They are being delivered in large numbers in commercial hardware and software distributions, unbeknownst to the organizations in the distribution chain. If this pattern continues unchecked, the ramifications may be dramatic.

Some in the virus defense industry claim that damage is already in the billions of dollars per year and climbing exponentially, while more conservative estimates place damages in the range of $1 per computer per year in industry (about $500 million dollars per year). No matter what the actual loss, this will clearly have a dramatic effect on the fabric of modern society as we become more and more dependent on less and less reliable information systems.

We are already seeing laws introduced around the world to protect computers from such attacks, which until a few years ago were not even illegal. New standards for computer systems and networks are being devised with integrity criteria as a central theme. University and government research has increased dramatically, and the topic is becoming more and more integrated into the everyday thinking of modern organizations.

10.4 The Best Hope Yet

Hardware and software to support integrity is a vital factor to long term integrity protection in information systems, and there are already sufficient techniques and products to allow a high degree of protection in most modern systems.

POset based systems and networks will have a dramatic impact on both the adequacy of protection and our ability to use available protection effectively. There are already some systems in the commercial market that dramatically reduce the complexity of protection mangement while assuring far greater assurance that available protection is properly used.

Integrity shells have started to become the dominant method of integrity protection against viruses in modern computer systems, and this technology will continue to dominate the integrity protection market for some time to come. The most important reason for the success of integrity shells is their cost effectiveness and the degree to which they have been integrated into the normal operating environment without requiring any significant expertise by the average user.

Education in information protection must increase if there is to be a long term hope for integrity in modern information systems. The educational system has been downright negligent in ignoring information protection as a topic. For example, the average university graduate in computer science has less than 15 minutes of education in information protection, while over 5% of the computing budget of most modern organizations is dedicated to this field, and according to sources in the insurance industry, nearly 4% of the GNP of most industrialized nations is lost each year due to integrity problems in computer systems.

Finally, we must start to view protection as an activity to be pursued throughout the organization, and not as a product that can be simply bought and forgotten.

Appendix A

The Good Joke

This is not my original joke, but I have told it after lunch at so many short courses, that it is an integral part of the course. I include it here for your pleasure. I first heard it told by a NIST (National Institute of Science and Technology) speaker at a computer virus conference I attended.

It seems that this guy was hired to work for one of the national security agencies in the United States and the guy that was in place before him left under some very serious controversy ... some problem with a computer network or something. So during the transition period, after the job related briefings, the old guy gave him three envelopes labeled 1, 2, and 3, with the instructions to put the three envelopes into the security safe and to only use them in the most dire of emergencies. Well, the new guy had no idea what these three envelopes were about, and the old guy wouldn't tell him, so he thought it was sort of strange, but he put them in the safe to satisfy the old guy, and forgot about them after a couple of months.

So after about a year in office, a major crisis came along. It was something to do with the US Embassy in Moscow. It seems the embassy was built by Soviet workmen, complete with built-in bugging

179

devices, and when the press found out about it, they called up the President. The President's office arranged for a press conference at 3:30 and called this guy and told him he had a press conference scheduled in 15 minutes to answer questions about the Moscow Embassy situation. Of course, this guy had no idea what was going on, but he figured he was in big trouble, and then recalled the three envelopes.

So he went down to the security safe, opened it up, took out the envelope labeled '1', locked up the safe, opened up the envelope, and read it. It said: "Blame it on your predecessor". Okay, he was desperate, and he didn't know what else to do, so he went to the press Conference and said: "I was not involved in the decision to build the embassy in this way, however my predecessor was involved in it and . . . We became aware of the situation several months before you did, and were working very hard to resolve it, and . . . ". The press ate it up. They blamed it on a previous administration, and our guy came out clean.

So he went on down the road, and about a year and a half later, son-of-a-gun if there wasn't another big problem. This time somebody in Germany launched a computer virus that spread through NASA networks into the United States, and the Press called the President, and the President called a press conference for 3:30, and informed our hero with about 15 minutes notice that he was to describe what happened with this NASA network.

Well, if it works once, you don't forget it, so our hero went down and got the second envelope out of the security safe, locked up the safe, opened up the envelope, and read it. It said "Blame it on the operating system". Why not? So our hero went to the press conference and said "The operating system in these computers are fundamentally weak, and our people have been aware of that for a number of years and have been working to resolve the problem . . . ". Well, the press ate it up, and our hero came out unscathed again.

After about another year and a half, it happened again. This time there was some sailor who worked in the US Department of Defense in classified areas, and this sailor was giving away keys to the cryptosystems used for nuclear missile control. So, the press called the President, and the President scheduled a press conference for 3:30, and called our hero with 15 minutes notice. So our guy figured he was in big trouble again, and decided to use the third envelope.

He went down to the security safe, got out the third envelope, locked up the safe, opened up the envelope, and read the last piece of paper. It said: "Prepare three envelopes".

Appendix B

Annotated Bibliography

- F. Cohen, "Computer Viruses - Theory and Experiments", DOD/NBS 7th Conference on Computer Security, originally appearing in IFIP-sec 84, also appearing in IFIP-TC11 "Computers and Security", V6(1987), pp22-35 and other publications in several languages. This is the most famous paper on computer viruses, and forms the basis for most of the current understanding of the field.

- J. P. Anderson, "Computer Security Technology Planning Study", USAF Electronic Systems Division, #ESD-TR-73-51, Oct 1972, (Cited in Denning). This study evaluated computer security issues that were prevalent prior to the introduction of the virus problem.

- R. R. Linde, "Operating System Penetration", AIFIPS National Computer Conference, pp 361-368, 1975. This paper described many of the common techniques for operating systems protection, and how systems could be designed to defend against them.

- D. E. Bell and L. J. LaPadula, "Secure Computer Systems: Mathematical Foundations and Model", The Mitre Corporation, 1973 (cited in many papers). This was the classic paper in which Bell and LaPadula described a model for maintaining secrecy in timesharing computer systems.

- D. E. Denning, "Cryptography and Data Security", Addison Wesley, 1982. This is a very good graduate text on computer security covering most of the important issues prior to computer viruses.

- E. J. McCauley and P. J. Drongowski, "KSOS - The Design of a Secure Operating System", AIFIPS National Computer Conference, pp 345-353, 1979. This paper describes one of the operating systems designed in the 1970s to maintain secrecy.

- G.J. Popek, M. Kampe, C.S. Kline, A. Stoughton, M. Urban, and E.J. Walton, "UCLA Secure Unix", AIFIPS, National Computer Conference 1979, pp355-364. This paper describes a secure implementation of the Unix operating system in which much of the implementation was proven correct mathematically.

- B. D. Gold, R. R. Linde, R. J. Peeler, M. Schaefer, J.F. Scheid, and P.D. Ward, "A Security Retrofit of VM/370", AIFIPS National Computer Conference, pp335-344, 1979. This paper describes some of the effort to make an insecure computer system secure through a major retrofit.

- C. E. Landwehr, "The Best Available Technologies for Computer Security", IEEE Computer, V16#7, July, 1983. This paper summarized computer security techniques and implementations up until the advent of computer viruses.

- B. W. Lampson, "A note on the Confinement Problem", Communications of the ACM V16(10) pp613-615, Oct, 1973. This famous paper described the covert channel problem for the first time.

- K. J. Biba, "Integrity Considerations for Secure Computer Systems", USAF Electronic Systems Division (cited in Denning), 1977. In this paper, the dual of the Bell LaPadula model is used to achieve integrity levels in a computer system for the first time.

- K. Thompson, "Reflections on Trusting Trust", Turing award lecture, 1984, CACM, Aug, 1984. This paper described the Thompson C compiler which allows Thompson to login to almost any Unix system.

- F. Cohen, "Computer Viruses", PhD Dissertation, University of Southern California, 1986, ASP Press (PO Box 81270, Pittsburgh, PA 15217 USA) This is a mathematical treatment of the computer virus issue, and contains the first formal definition of viruses, many of the proofs about defenses, and much of the basis for current computer virus theory.

- A. Dewdney, "Computer Recreations", Scientific American, 1984-1986. This is a series of articles about computer games involving competing programs in an environment. It turns out that the most successful ones tend to be viruses.

- F. Cohen, "Computer Security Methods and Systems", 1984 Conference on Information Systems and Science, Princeton University, 1984 This paper describes much of the computer security technology prior to viruses.

- M. Pozzo and T. Gray, "Managing Exposure to Potentially Malicious Programs", Proceedings of the 9th National Computer Security Conference, Sept. 1986. This paper describes a "trusted software" approach to computer virus defense, where in software is given different levels of trust and information flow is limited based on these levels.

- F. Cohen, "A Secure Computer Network Design", IFIP-TC11 Computers and Security, V4#3, Sept. 1985, pp 189-205, also appearing in AFCEA Symp. and Expo. on Physical and Electronic Security, Aug. 1985 This paper describes the combination of the Bell-LaPadula and Biba models, extends previous results to computer networks, and introduces some major insecurities in computer networks.

- F. Cohen, "Protection and Administration of Information Networks Under Partial Orderings", IFIP-TC11 Computers and Security, V6(1987) pp118-128. In this paper, the use of POsets to describe protection in a computer system is introduced. Collusion analysis is developed, and several examples are given.

- F. Cohen, "Design and Administration of Distributed and Hierarchical Information Networks Under Partial Orderings", IFIP-TC11 Computers and Security, V6(1987), 15 pages. In this paper, previous results are extended to cover management of distributed and hierarchical networks. Protocols for distributed POset protection are given, and previous analysis is extended.

- M. Pozzo and T. Gray, "Computer Virus Containment in Untrusted Computing Environments", IFIP/SEC 4th International Conference on Computers and Security, Dec. 1986. In this paper, a cryptographic technique based on public key cryptography is given for implementing trusted software as a protection mechanism.

- F. Cohen, "Design and Administration of an Information Network Under a Partial Ordering - A Case Study", IFIP-TC11 Computers and Security, V6(1987) pp332-338. In this paper, a case study of a POset based protection system is described. Results indicated that implementation and use were both easier with the increased structure, and tracking down the sources of corruption was greatly improved.

- F. Cohen, "Designing Provably Correct Information Networks with Digital Diodes", IFIP-TC11 Computers and Security, 1988. This paper describes a hardware device for highly reliable one-way transmission so as to facilitate hardware based POset implementations.

- F. Cohen, "A Cryptographic Checksum for Integrity Protection in Untrusted Computer Systems", IFIP-TC11 Computers and Security, V6(1987). This paper introduced a cryptographic method for protecting the integrity of information stored on disk by providing reliable detection of change.

- F. Cohen, "Two Secure Network File Servers", IFIP-TC11, Computers and Security, 1987. This paper describes two prototype implementations of POset based file servers designed to facilitate POset based networks.

- M. Pozzo and T. Gray, "An Approach to Containing Computer Viruses", IFIP-TC11 Computers and Security, 1987. This paper describes a novel approach to computer virus containment through cryptographic signatures.

- B. Cohen and F. Cohen, "Error Prevention at a Radon Measurement Service Laboratory", Radiation Protection Management, V6#1, pp43-47, Jan. 1989. This paper describes a high integrity computing environment in which dramatic increases in integrity were attained at very low cost.

- F. Cohen, "A Complexity Based Integrity Maintenance Mechanism", Conference on Information Sciences and Systems, Princeton University, March 1986. This paper first described the concept of software self-defense and proposed an implementation based on cryptographic checksumming techniques.

- F. Cohen, "Recent Results in Computer Viruses", Conference on Information Sciences and Systems, Johns Hopkins University, March 1985. This paper summarized early results on computer viruses and defenses.

- F. Cohen, "Maintaining a Poor Person's Integrity", IFIP-TC11 Computers and Security, 1987. This paper describes methods by which people without much financial support could protect themselves from computer viruses through pure;y procedural methods.

- W. Murray, "The Application of Epidemiology to Computer Viruses", Computers and Security, Computers and Security, 1989. This paper details some interesting work in modeling computer viruses and defenses based on biological methods.

- H. Highland - ED, Special Issue of "Computers and Security", April, 1988, IFIP TC-11. This was the first special issue on computer viruses in a scientific journal, and included several good papers on the topic.

- V. McLellan, "Computer Systems Under Seige", The New York Times, Sunday, Jan. 31, 1988. This was one of the early articles on computer viruses in the popular press.

- J F Shoch and J A Hupp, "The 'Worm' Programs - Early Experience with a Distributed Computation", CACM pp172-180, March, 1982. This was a famous paper that first described the Xerox "worm" experiments for parallel processing on a distributed computing network.

- J.B. Gunn, "Use of Virus Functions to Provide a Virtual APL Interpreter Under User Control", CACM, pp163-168, July, 1974. This paper describes a "viral" technique for modifying the APL interpreter, but did not involve replication or infection.

- L. J. Hoffman, "Impacts of information system vulnerabilities on society", AIFIPS National Computer Conference, pp461-467, 1982. This paper describes the degree to which we have become dependent on computer systems and what we could reasonably expect to result from existing system vulnerabilities.

- Kaplan, [U.S. Dept. of Justice, Bureau of Justice Statistics] "Computer Crime - Computer Security Techniques", U.S. Government Printing Office, Washington, DC, 1982. This is a wonderful resource book on computer security techniques, and gives a firm basis for EDP audit from the pre-virus era.

- M. H. Klein, "Department of Defense Trusted Computer System Evaluation Criteria", Department of Defense Computer Security Center, Fort Meade, Md. 20755, 1983 DOD-CSC-84-001. This is the widely touted "orange book" Trusted System Evaluation Criteria published by the NSA for evaluating multilevel secure systems for military use. Although it has become a de-facto standard, it does not address integrity or many other issues widely held to be of more widespread import.

- A. Turing, "On Computable Numbers, with an Application to the Entscheidungsproblem", London Math Soc Ser 2, 1936.

This is the famous paper that shows that any problem that can be solved by any general purpose computer can also be solved by any other general purpose computer, given enough time and space.

- S. Yau and R. Cheung, "Design of Self Checking Software", Conference on Reliable Software, IEEE, 1975, pp450-457. This is one of a series of papers on software based fault tolerant computing.

- J. Kelly and A. Avizienis, "A Specification Oriented Multi-Version Software Experiment", IEEE Symposium on Fault Tolerant Computing pp120-126, 1983. This paper describes some of the major problems with multi-version programming and the experiments performed at UCLA to evaluate its potential for practical use.

- R. Scott, J. Gault, D. McAllister, and J. Wiggs, "Experimental Validation of Six Fault Tolerant Software Reliability Models", IEEE Symposium on Fault Tolerant Computing, pp102-107, 1984. This paper advances the practice of multi-version programming by showing the importance of good specification to the final outcome.

- L. Chen and A. Avizienis, "N-version programming: a fault tolerance approach to reliability of software operation", FTCS-8, pp 3-9, June, 1978. This paper introduced the N-version programming model.

- L. Chen, "Improving Software Reliability by N-version Programming", UCLA Computer Science Dept, UCLA-ENG-7843, 1978. This paper described some improvements to the initial work on N-version programming.

- Randell, "System Structure for Software Fault Tolerance", IEEE Transactions on Software Engineering, June 1975, pp220-223, Vol.SE-1. This paper introduces the systems requirements for reliable N-version software implementations.

- M. Harrison, W. Ruzzo, and J. Ullman, "Protection in Operating Systems", CACM V19#8, Aug 1976, pp461-471. This paper introduces the first formal mathematical model of protection in computer systems, and forms the basis for the Subject/Object model of computer security. It also proves that determining the protection effects of a given configuration is, in general, undecidable.

- M. Cohen, "A New Integrity Based Model for Limited Protection Against Computer Viruses", Masters Thesis, The Pennsylvania State University, College Park, PA 1988. This thesis describes the concept of integrity shells as a method of defending against computer viruses.

- F. Cohen, "Models of Practical Defenses Against Computer Viruses", IFIP-TC11, "Computers and Security", V7#6, December, 1988. This paper formally introduces integrity shells and shows that they are optimal as a defense against computer viruses.

- F. Cohen, "Automated Integrity Maintenance for Viral Defense", IFIP-TC11, "Computers and Security", 1990. This paper describes some of the automated decision making issues in the use of integrity shells for a computer virus defense.

- DPMA 2nd annual computer virus symposium, New York, NY, 1989. This conference had several interesting papers on vulnerabilities in computer systems and computer virus defenses.

- S. Jones and C. White Jr., "The IPM Model of Computer Virus Management", IFIP-TC11, (submitted 1989). This model of management issues in computer virus defense considers viruses as pests in an agricultural environment.

- F. Cohen, "The ASP 3.0 Technical Users Manual", ASP Press, 1990 (PO Box 81270, Pittsburgh PA 15217, USA). This is the technical manual for the first commercial integrity shell.

- F. Cohen, "ASP 3.0 - The Integrity Shell", Information Protection, V1#1, January 1990, ASP Press, 1990 (PO Box 81270, Pittsburgh PA 15217, USA). This article describes some of the issues in integrity shells as a practical defense against viruses without using any high powered mathematics.

- Y. J. Huang and F. Cohen, "Some Weak Points of One Fast Cryptographic Checksum Algorithm and its Improvement", IFIP-TC11 "Computers and Security", V8#1, February, 1989. This paper shows several weaknesses in one cryptographic checksum used as a viral defense, and shows how it can be improved.

- M. Prew, "Minimizing the Impact of Computer Crime on your Earnings", Wigham Poland (Corporation of Lloyds), 1984. This article was written by an insurance underwriter to describe the economic impacts of computer crime in modern society.

- H. Highland, "Computer Virus Handbook", Elsevier, 1990. This is a very good book on computer viruses from a technological standpoint, and covers much of the basis for present computer virus theory as well. It is recommended reading for those interested in computer viruses under the DOS operating system.

- S. White, "A Status Report on IBM Computer Virus Research", Italian Computer Virus Conference, 1990. This paper describes the status of computer virus research at IBM's high integrity computing laboratory.

- L. Adleman, "An Abstract Theory of Computer Viruses", "Lecture Notes in Computer Science", V403, Advances in Computing - Proceedings of Crypto-88, S. Goldwasser, Ed., Springer-Verlag, 1990. This was the second theoretical work on computer viruses, describes a subset of the previous formal definition, and demonstrates that detection of members of this subset is also undecidable.

- E. Spafford, "Crisis and Aftermath", CACM, V32#6, June, 1989. This is one of the short papers published in a special issue of CACM on the computer virus attack on the internet.

- J. Rochlis and M. Eichin, "With Microscope and Tweezers: The Worm from MIT's Perspective", CACM, V32#6, June, 1989. This is another paper describing the efforts to fight the Internet virus from the ACM special issue on the virus in the internet.

- F. Cohen, "Some Simple Advances in Protection Tools", Information Protection, V1#5-9, June-Oct 1990, ASP Press (PO Box 81270, Pittsburgh PA 15217, USA). This article describes some of the simple advances in protection tools needed to facilitate proper management of the enormous amount of protection state in modern computer systems.

- W. Gleissner, "A Mathematical Theory for the Spread of Computer Viruses", "Computers and Security", IFIP TC-11, V8#1, Jan. 1989 pp35-41. This paper gives a thorough mathematical analysis of the spread of computer viruses in computer systems, including predictions of spread times based on various properties of system use.

- Tipet, "The Tipet Theory of Computer Virus Propagation", Foundationware, USA. This is a very oversimplified model of viral spread that predicts enormous global calamity if viruses go unchecked.

- C. Shannon, "A Mathematical Theory of Communications", Bell Systems Technical Journal, 1949. This classic paper describes information theory for the first time, and forms the basis for all of modern syntactic information theory. It also shows that covert channels (as well as any other channels) can be arbitrarily reliable even in the presence of purposely introduced noise.

- F. Cohen, "Current Best Practice Against PC Integrity Corruption", Information Protection, V1#1, January 1990, ASP Press (PO Box 81270, Pittsburgh PA 15217). This paper describes procedural requirements for sound computer virus defense in PC based environments.

- F. Cohen, "Computer Viruses", chapter in "Computers Under Attack", ACM/Addison Wesley (1990). This is a good summary of computer virus research results, but is redundant once you have read this book.

- F. Cohen, "The Impact of Information Protection on Computer Engineering", Information Protection, V1#4, April, 1990, ASP Press, (PO Box 81270, Pittsburgh PA 15217). This paper describes the degree to which protection issues has influenced the basic design of computer systems.

- F. Cohen, "How To Do Sound Change Control and What It Costs", Information Protection, V1#6, June, 1990, ASP Press, (PO Box 81270, Pittsburgh PA 15217). This paper describes the cost of sound change control.

- H. Gliss, "The Security of Information Resources - Results of a Survey", The Oxbridge Sessions, Holland, 1990. This paper gives the results of one of the best computer security surveys ever completed in industry.

- F. Cohen, "A Cost Analysis of Typical Computer Viruses and Defenses", IFIP-TC11, "Computers and Security", (submitted, 1990). This paper describes the mathematical analysis of the costs of computer virus defenses, and shows that integrity shells are far more cost effective than other competitive techniques currently in the environment.

- M. Pozzo, Ph.D. Dissertation, University of California at Los Angeles, 1990. This thesis describes essentially ineffective attempts at trying to find computer viruses by examining executable programs and trying to predict their behavior. It also contains a number of intersting advances in the use of public key cryptography and proof of program correctness for viral defense.

- J. Hirst, "Eliminator - Computer Virus Detection and Removal", Copyright (c), British Computer Virus Research Centre, 1990. This shows the state-of-the-art in special purpose automated computer virus detection and removal.

- L. Hoffman, "Rogue Programs - Viruses, Worms, and Trojan Horses" Von Noisted, Reinhold, 1990. This book is a good resource for papers on computer viruses and related integrity attacks against modern computers.

- G. Davida, Y. Desmedt, and B. Matt, "Defending Against Computer Viruses through Cryptographic Authentication", 1989 IEEE Symposium on Computer Security and Privacy, pp 312-

318. This paper is a minor extension of previous results on integrity protection through cryptographic checksums.

- M. Joseph and A. Avizienis, "A Fault Tolerance Approach to Computer Viruses", 1988 IEEE Symposium on Security and Privacy, April, 1988. In this paper, extensions to software fault tolerance are applied to computer virus defense in critical systems.

Addendum

Since the first publication of this book, there have been several changes in the world virus situation, advances in virus defense, and other issues that have come to light. In future printings, we hope to integrate this information into the text, but for now, we have decided to include this addendum to keep you as up-to-date as possible.

More and More Viruses

In early 1990, there were about 125 real-world computer viruses known to the research community, and a new one was appearing at the rate of about 1 every 6 days. Unfortunately, things have changed for the worse. As of early 1991, there were about 600 known viruses, and a new one was appearing more than once per day. In late 1991, there are about 1,000 viruses known to members of the research community. As corroborating evidence, in 1989 relatively few companies attending my talks claimed virus experiences, while as of late 1991, almost every company I encounter claims to have experienced several viruses in the last year.

Although many of these viruses have not spread widely, the number of widespread viruses is on the increase, and the incidence level is increasing quickly. For example, in a recent visit to Taiwan, I was surprised to learn that of 50 companies represented at a seminar, on the average they experienced about 10 viruses per year! This is particularly important in light of the fact that most [1] of the world's **PCs** are manufactured in Taiwan, and several incidents of widespread dissemination of viruses from the manufacturer have been reported.

These numbers, however, are only the tip of the iceberg. They represent very substantial growth, but don't reflect the recent advances in attack technology. Several virus generating programs

---

[1] I heard the figure of 80%, but I cannot confirm it.

1

are currently available, both from semi-legitimate software houses, and from other less identifiable sources. These virus generators are capable of generating many thousands of different viruses automatically, and in some cases, allow the user to select from different infection techniques, triggering mechanisms, damage, etc. Even simple evolution through self modification is available in some of these generators.

A far more interesting program has been developed to perform automated evolution of existing programs so as to create numerous equivalent but different programs. This program exploits knowledge of program structure, equivalence of large classes of instructions, and sequential independence of unrelated instructions to replace the sequence of instructions comprising a program with a behaviorally equivalent instruction sequence which is substantially different in appearance and operation from the original. Let's look at examples with part of a 'C' program:

```
i=10;j=12;k=17;for (l=0;l<i;l++,j++) k=k+j*i;
```

As an example of restructuring, we can systematically add or alter function calls to replace existing structures with structures which produce equivalent results in a different manner as follows:

```
int zz(x) int x; {return(x-4);}
int yy(x) int x; {return(x+1);}
{int jj;jj=0;i=10;jj++;}
k=zz(21);j=k-5;
for (l=0;l<i;l=yy(l),j=yy(j)) k=k+j*i;
```

Statement equivalence can be exploited by replacing existing statements with replacements which yield the same result even though they operate quite differently as follows:

```
int zz(x) int x;{int j,k; j=x-20;k=j+16;return(k);}
```

2

```
int yy(x) int x;{return(x*2-(x-1));}
{int jj,kk;kk=1;jj=0;i=2*5;jj=jj+kk;}
k=zz((7*6)<<1);j=k-(25/5);l=0;
while(l<i) {k=k+j*i;l=yy(l);j=yy(j));}
```

Statement reordering involves finding sequences of instructions
that can be reordered without impacting program results. It turns
out that every program can be represented as a POset which describes the dependence of each statement on all previous statements. When order independence exists, reordering is possible
without impacting operation. This technique is used to analyze
programs for parallelization, but can also be used to evolve programs in other ways. Here is an example of a reordering of the
example:

```
int yy(x) int x;{return(x*2-(x-1));}
int zz(x) int x;{int k,j; j=x-20;k=j+16;return(k);}
j=k-(25/5);k=zz((7*6)<<1);l=0;
{int kk,jj;jj=0;i=2*5;kk=1;jj=jj+kk;}
while(l<i) {k=k+j*i;j=yy(j));l=yy(l);}
```

Now let's compare this to the original program to get an idea
of how different it looks when we apply all of these techniques in
sequence:

```
i=10;j=12;k=17;for (l=0;l<i;l++,j++) k=k+j*i;
```

Clearly, the final program is quite different from the original.
We can also change variable names and perform other cosmetic
changes that impact the source code appearance, but these are unlikely to impact the compiled version of the program substantially.

This evolution is of course only at the 'C' source code level. The
same procedures can be used at lower levels to evolve the assembly
level program. The net effect is a program with almost identical

3

performance and identical results, but quite different operation, representation, and appearance.

In our experiments, we were able to evolve a 100 line 'C' program of about the same complexity as a typical virus in a few seconds on a **PC**. Thus we could easily create 15,000 equivalent viruses a day. Non-equivalent viruses can also be evolved by selecting code segments from interoperable evolution, infection, triggering, and damage routines as was demonstrated in the 'Even Worse' virus described earlier. We have created an experimental algorithm capable of generating $O(n!)$ different viruses at the rate of several per minute.

It seems that we have entered a new era of viral attack, wherein the simplistic defenses that were marginally acceptable in the past are now of far less value. For example, a typical virus scanner that scans for over 600 known viruses takes over 10 minutes to scan a typical hard disk on a **PC**. I recently went to a computer store to look at a 486/40Mhz computer with a 1Gbyte disk, and was surprised to see a virus scanner included with the system. On bootup, this system took over 20 minutes to perform the scan, and could not be interrupted. I finally gave up on testing the system, and I have a lot of tolerance for virus defenses. Clearly, a 20 minute delay at every bootup is beyond the normal expectation of a computer user.

Theories of Viral Spread

Some recent work has concentrated on analyzing viral spread with an eye toward figuring out how many systems will be infected over time. There are basically 4 theories currently being considered.

- Probably the most detailed theory on viral spread was first published in 1989 by W. Gleissner. This theory appears to accurately parameterize the problem and its solution, but is

4

widely ignored (probably) because it requires more mathematical sophistication to apply than most people are willing to use, and the parameters required for the analysis are hard to derive. It also makes some assumptions about uniformity that may not reflect the real world situation.

- In 1990, Peter Tippet proposed the 'Tippet' theory of viral spread that assumes exponential growth and uniform global sharing. According to the Tippet predictions, we should have far more viruses today than we actually have, and most serious researchers discounted this theory early as being too simplistic. Exponential growth is an obvious characteristic of replicating systems which was suggested in the first virus papers, but there are limits on this growth that must be considered for a realistic theory.

- The theory of epidemics has been around for quite some time. It now appears that this theory is quite good at predicting behavior in closed environments with uniform communication properties. In this theory, the number of new infections depends on the number of previous infections, their probability of performing infection given the available uninfected population, and the communication and execution rates. As more programs become infected in the early stages of a disease, the growth is essentially exponential, but as more programs become infected, the number of uninfected programs available for infection shrinks, and eventually dwindles. This is called saturation.

  When we add cure (or death), we get a situation where a cure rate can dominate an infection rate. As more infected programs live in the environment, the infection rate grows until a level of 'epidemic' is reached above which the infection rate exceeds the cure rate and all programs that can become infected become infected.

  This theory has been extended to include the impact of spread between less connected communities, inoculations, and immunity as well as other biologically relevant issues.

- The research group at IBM's high integrity computing laboratory has developed another model for viral spread (published in the IEEE Oakland conference on computer security, 1991), wherein they extend the two-level theory of epidemics to a hierarchical model and consider the impact of detection, eradication, and system failure due to viruses.

  In essence, they buy into exponential growth for small numbers of viruses in large populations of PCs with homogeneous sharing, but if (as seems reasonable), spread is not homogeneous, their hierarchical model shows spread rates to be dependent on connectivity. If each node in the network connects to only 2 other nodes (i.e. a linear array of communicating organizations), you would expect that each time step would only yield the new infection of two more organizations. For a square grid, you would expect growth as $time^2$, for an n-cube, you would expect growth as $time^n$, etc. When a Poison distribution of virus scanner use is added, and assuming only known viruses are present, the problem may be far less critical than previously concluded.

  Their hierarchical model currently ignores some types of communication such as those leading to widespread distribution of viruses from manufacturers, and assumes that virus scanning happens at uniformly distributed times. Thus the results are significantly different than those that would result from daily scanning.

If we are to look at this scientifically, the final judgement in any analysis of viral spread has to be the experimental evidence. If we had enough data and information about parameters, we could test each of the theories, but we do not, and because of a general lack of sufficient audit trails, it is unlikely that anyone will get accurate figures soon. No substantial instrumentation has been reported since the original tests performed in 1984.

I personally buy into the theory of epidemics as a good predictive technique in the large, but it is inaccurate when non-uniform communication boundaries exist, which is often the case in computer systems. It also does not cover the 'typhoid Mary' case very well, and this seems to be very important in computer viruses, since it appears that most of the widespread sharing is through these social users. The IBM extension to this theory currently ignores too many important cases to be broadly useful, but is still under development, and is likely to become far more accurate over time.

New Viral Defense Techniques

A lot of the following discussions pertains primarily to **PC** architectures at this time, but has broader applications. We apologize ahead of time for this concentration, but since **PC**s are the dominant architecture in the world at this time, and since **PC** viruses dominate all others by more than a factor of 10, it does not seem inappropriate to look at the problem from this perspective.

In an environment where the first program to run has total control of the computer, in theory, it cannot be bypassed. It could, for example, simulate the remainder of the machine, and thus avoid any technique for defense that a defender could put in place. This works both for the attacker and the defender, but on a **PC** the floppy disk, by default, is the boot device, so it really applies to the last disk from which the system was bootstrapped.

In almost every current computer, this situation holds, but the performance impact of such a thorough simulation is almost guaranteed to be noticed by the user. It is normal to have at least a factor of 10 reduction in performance in simulated operation. In a system with operating system protection, much better performance can be attained, because the protected mode program only need simulate instructions which violate the restricted memory or instruction space provided to 'user' programs. The processor takes care of the remainder of the processing. Even other programs' protected mode instructions can be simulated if the attacker is clever enough.

In practice, attackers are not yet doing this well. The best of the simulation viruses (typically called 'stealth viruses' because they simulate an uninfected system) are placed in the partition table of the **PC**, which is the first programmable sequence of instructions executed by the machine on hard-disk bootstrap. In some new hardware systems, even the system 'ROM's are programmable (PROMs), and these may be modified by experts to include a virus at or below the BIOS level of operation, but this is not yet widespread. Several new defenses have been designed to address the increasing number of partition table 'stealth' viruses in the environment. The most general techniques are the 'BootLock' and 'SnapShot' methods.

In addition to containing the first instructions to be executed, the partition table includes information on how the disk is structured. A 'BootLock' program replaces the default partition table program with a program that loads the partition table from elsewhere on the disk. This limits access to the disk by replacing the normal disk descriptor with a descriptor that cannot be understood by **DOS**, which in turn makes the use of **DOS** to modify the partition table infeasible. It may also replace the hardware installed locations used by the operating system to access disk areas, and thus prevent modification of the partition table except through the floppy disk bootstrap process.

Some current partition table viruses use ROM locations to directly access disk hardware, and they can thus corrupt the physical partition table, but they still cannot be used to examine or modify the logical contents of the **DOS** disk. This means that unless attackers use defense specific attacks, they cannot reasonably be expected to infect **DOS** files. Thus BootLock protection prevents all but low-level viruses from entering the system when bootstrapped from the floppy disk.

8

The 'SnapShot' defense makes a copy of the memory, registers, and other critical operating information at first use, and replaces the memory state of the machine with the stored state on subsequent uses. This has the effect of removing any corruption from memory at system startup, and thus provides an uninfected initial state for checking and repairing the remainder of the system, including the partition table and operating system critical files.

Assuming this mechanism gets control, it can defeat any memory resident attack, and bypass even the most clever simulation virus. The only ways around this defense are a defense-specific attack or a high quality system simulation by the virus. In the race between attack and defense, viruses that bypass this mechanism must use far more space and time than current viruses, and likely represents an increase in viral complexity by several orders of magnitude over today's state-of-the-art.

There are also several weak defenses that exploit assumptions made by attackers to make substantial numbers of current viral attacks fail. For example, we can prevent 'executable' programs from being modified in-place by limiting 'open' calls on files with particular names. It turns out that this defense prevents infection by over 90% of current **PC** viruses, while consuming only about 20 instructions on each file 'open', and not impacting most normal operation. This is a weak defense because, for example, the attacker could rename the file, perform infection, and rename it back after infection, without impacting this mechanism. We can limit renames, but this is also easily bypassed. If we make this protection too effective, the system becomes too constrained for normal use.

Another weak defense is a mechanism that prevents tracing through operating system calls. It turns out that many viruses trace calls into the operating system to determine internal operating system addresses which are then used to bypass protection. We can stop most of these attacks by turning off tracing at an appropriate point in the defense. This attack can be defeated by a sufficiently cleaver attacker by simply checking defense operations to determine if they turn off tracing, and simulating the instructions that turn tracing off. The **DOS** debugger does this to some extent, and the techniques it uses can be augmented to cover more clever trace trapping defenses.

Several other weak defenses are now in common use, and to the extent that they consume very few system resources while defending against substantial portions of the existing attack techniques, they are valuable and cost effective, particularly in the short run. For the most part, these very weak defenses have utility because the operating system has weak protection. With sound operating system protection, these attacks are ineffective, so the defenses are unnecessary.

Defense-in-depth Against Viruses

Defense-in-depth redundantly combines techniques that are individually less than ideal, to provide a whole defense that is, presumably, stronger than any of its components. For example, all of the techniques we have discussed in this book can coexist without difficulty.

Defense-in-depth also leads to synergistic effects that may cause each of the defenses to operate with more strength than it could operate with alone. It turns out that the combination of POset based access control with an integrity shell is particularly important. Without integrity protection, we have seen that access control becomes ineffective, while without access control, integrity protection is subject to corruption of the defense mechanism. When they are combined, they offer both integrity for the access control scheme and alteration defense for the integrity mechanism.

Another advantage of defense-in-depth is that it permits the defender to compensate for new attacks before they succeed in completely penetrating the defense, even when they are partially successful. For example, a previously unknown virus will bypass the virus monitor, but may be detected by the integrity shell. We can then augment the virus monitor to defend against this attack without intervening exposures due to the inadequacy of the monitor. As new viruses are detected and defended by the combined defense, each of the component defenses are improved, so similar viruses don't penetrate as far in the future.

Several implementations of defense-in-depth for **DOS** have been developed and tested, and are currently in widespread use. As of this time, over 200 new viruses have been introduced into one such defense without the defense breaking down. Eventually, any defense can be defeated, but the use of defense-in-depth seems to provide far more effective protection than any other current alternatives.

Benevolent Virus Potentials

On March 22, 1991, the world high speed computing record was broken by a Massachusetts company specializing in parallel processing. The previous record holder, contrary to popular belief, was the Internet virus. The design flaw that caused unchecked growth demonstrates one of the malicious aspects of this virus, and unfortunately, many of the other computer viruses we hear about are also malicious, but like any new technology, viruses are a two edged sword.

Consider that the Internet Virus performed about 32 million operations per second on each of 6,000 computers, and another 3.2 million operations per second on each of 60,000 computers, for a grand total of 384 Billion operations per second! It took hundreds of person-years of work and millions of dollars to design the computer hardware and software that broke this processing record, while the Internet Virus was written by one graduate student using existing computers in his spare time over a period of a few months. For pure processing cycles, computer viruses are some of the fastest distributed programs we know of, but unfortunately, we haven't yet grown enough scientifically or ethically to exploit their vast potential.

The same issues that make viruses a serious threat to computer integrity make them a powerful mechanism for reliable and efficient distribution of computation. They distribute freely, easily, and evenly throughout a computing environment; they provide for general purpose computerized problem solving; and they are very reliable even in environments where computer systems fail quite often.

Efficient uniform distribution of computing between computers working together on the same problem is one of the hardest problems we face in parallel processing. For large parallel processors working on complex problems, it is often more difficult to find an optimal way to distribute problem solving among available computers than it is to do the problem solving once the processing is distributed. With computer viruses, we automatically get distribution based on available processing for many computations because computers with less available processing tend to be slower to replicate viruses, while computers with more available processing tend to provide faster replication. Since viruses can spread wherever information spreads and is interpreted, viruses can eventually distribute themselves throughout networks regardless of how the computers are interconnected as long as they have general purpose function, transitive communication, and sharing. These two features eliminate the need to spend time figuring out how to distribute processing across computers in many applications.

Although general purpose problem solving is rarely a problem in computers today, reliability is particularly critical to large parallel processing applications because as the number of computers involved in problem solving increase, the likelihood of a failure during processing also increases. The Internet virus continued processing even though many systems in the Internet were turned off and many subnetworks were disconnected in an effort to stop it. Few modern parallel processing applications could continue processing in this sort of environment. In fact, most parallel processing computers today could produce erroneous results without even producing an error message, much less processing correctly when some of the computers fail. Viruses on the other hand have inherent reliability because of their ability to replicate and spread. Most of the computer viruses we know about work correctly in a wide variety of computer makes and models, work in both networks and isolated systems, work in many different versions of operating systems, spread to backup tapes and are revived when backups are restored, work on floppy-disks, hard-disks, and network pseudo-disks, and survive system failures and reconfigurations. Some of them even operate across different operating systems and types of computers.

Efficient and reliable distribution of processing in itself is not enough for efficient problem solving. For some problems, we have to be able to communicate results between processing components, while in other problems the time required for processing may be too small to justify the time required for distribution. The problem of controlling virus growth must be addressed before widespread use of viruses in existing computer networks will become acceptable to the user community, and evolution of viruses over time will probably be a vital component to their long term utility. Many issues in viral computation are not yet resolved, but there is also a substantial body of knowledge and experience to draw from.

The use of self-replicating programs for parallel processing is not new. In fact, John vonNeumann, one of the pioneers of the computer age, described reliable self-replicating programs in the 1940s. In many early works, the 'living' computer program was not just a distant possibility, but the intent of the exercise. Early papers talked of 'making reliable organisms out of unreliable organs', and 'intelligent self-organizing systems with numerous components'. Over the last 50 years, many authors have reported isolated experiments, and slow progress has been made.

Worms, Viruses, and Artificial Life

In 1982, a series of successful experiments with parallel processing used self-replicating programs that spread through the Xerox computer network. These so-called 'worm' programs would install 'segments' on computers which were not in use, each solving some part of the computation. Whenever a user wanted to use a computer, they pressed a 'reboot' button, and normal operation resumed. During the day, the worm would be trimmed back, running only on a few computers that were not in use, but at night, it would become active all over the network, performing tens of millions of useful calculations per second. Unfortunately, an error in one copy of the worm ended their experiments by causing the global Xerox network to reboot to the worm instead of the normal operating system. The entire network had to be restarted. A number of worm programs were also run on the Arpanet during the 1970s, some of them even capable of limited replication. For unspecified reasons, worm researchers apparently stopped performing these experiments in the early 1980s.

In 1984, the first experiments with 'Computer Viruses' as we know them today were performed. These 'Viruses' had many implications for integrity maintenance in computer systems, and were shown to be quite dangerous, but their potential for good was also introduced. A practical virus which reduced disk usage in exchange for increased startup time was described, and this technique that is now commonplace in personal computer systems. This work also pointed out the close link between computer viruses and other living systems, and even melded them into a unified mathematical theory of 'life' and its relationship to its environment. These experiments were terminated rather forcefully because they were so successful at demonstrating the inadequacy of contemporary computer security techniques, that administrators came to fear the implications.

In the mid 1980s, Scientific American began publishing a series on a mathematical 'game' called 'core wars', in which two or more competing programs struggled for survival in a simulated computer, while the game of 'Life' which simulates 'living cells' in a cellular automata has existed for quite a long time. To the extent that they replicate and/or evolve within the environment, they meet the mathematical definition of a computer virus. These examples of viruses have met with no significant resistance in the research community, presumably because they have no widespread impact.

In 1987, the first 'Artificial Life' conference was held, with researchers gathering from around the world to present papers on a loosely knit combination of many independent research areas that seek to describe, simulate, analyze, or implement living or life-like systems. In recent years artificial life has received increased attention both in the popular and the scientific communities, partly because of the emergence of computer viruses in modern computer networks, partly because of the growing number of interested researchers with results to report, and partly because of the efforts of some members of the research community who have started to make communication between divergent fields easier by providing common venues for publication and interaction.

The Viral Bill Collector

One useful computer virus is the automated 'bill collector', a virus that operates in a specially designed computing environment. Two such bill collectors have been implemented under the Unix operating system, one for a small business with thousands of orders of only a few hundred dollars each, and the other for a law office that specializes in collecting unpaid commercial loans for thousands of clients with tens of thousands of debtors. Taking the law office as an example, the computing environment 'births' a new bill collector every time a new case is entered by a user, kills bill collectors whenever the user indicates that a bill is fully paid or the case is abandoned, and allows the bill collector to write letters and evolve through its life-cycle.

In its simplest form, each bill collector is just a small program that collects a single bill by sending a series of letters over time depending on real-world events or the lack thereof as indicated by the user. It turns out that writing a computer program to collect a single bill is not very hard to do. In fact, in a few hours, an average programmer can write a simple bill collecting program that will do a pretty good job of collecting a single bill, based on the methods of collection used by an expert human bill collector.

If we were writing a high volume collection system in the standard fashion, we would implement a complex database management system. Next, we would devise a technique for scanning through this database periodically to determine which collection cases required action at any given time, and based on this list, have the bill collection program perform collections on all applicable cases. To collect statistics and resolve the status of cases, we would then have to implement another database scanning system, and the list goes on and on. By the time we are done, we have a very large and complex system.

With the viral programming approach, we take another tactic altogether. Instead of creating a large centralized bureaucracy which controls and directs all activities, we distribute all functions to the individual bill collectors. Each bill collector only has information related to its own collection case and the ability to selectively call upon its various scenarios for bill collection. Instead of scanning a database for bills to be collected, each bill collector schedules a 'wake up' call for the next time it has to do something. If some outside activity like a payment or a response to a previous action takes place, the human operators 'wake up' the appropriate bill collector by sending it the new information. The collector then reacts to the situation by 'evolving' its state and line of pursuit to meet the new situation, reschedules its pending wake up calls, and goes back to sleep.

One major advantage of writing a simple virus for this task is that all we have to do is provide basic replication, evolution, and wake up call mechanisms, and we don't have to deal with the complexity of large databases or long database searches to determine when to do what. Another major advantage is that since we are running many very small and independent programs instead of one large program, we can more easily distribute the computing load over a multitude of machines, and we don't have to deal with issues like simultaneous access, file locking, and process blocking.

There are also disadvantages, in that collecting data from all of the bill collectors is somewhat less efficient than looking up all of the data in a common database, and making changes to all of the independent bill collectors requires a systemic evolution process. To collect global data with a viral bill collector, we typically awaken every bill collector, ask for the required information, and collate the results. We end up writing several such data collection applications which we then schedule for operation in off hours. The results from the previous day are then always available the next morning, and since we are usually using otherwise idle computer time during off-peak hours, the inefficiency is not unduly bothersome. In an emergency, we can awaken all of the bill collectors during the day to get more instantaneous results, but in this case system wide performance suffers greatly. This feverish sort of activity is only required in the rarest of circumstances.

The advantages of the viral approach are even clearer in a networked environment. In a network, viruses self-distribute efficiently by replicating in remote processors. We can use performance as a survival criterion, or simply distribute performance information to viruses about to replicate in order to help balance the load. There are no shared data problems as in a distributed database because all of the data associated with each virus is local to that virus. When global data is requested, we get maximum parallelism for a significant portion of the process because the only bottleneck is in the reporting of results, which in the case of the bill collector takes relatively little bandwidth.

To evolve all of the independent bill collectors in response to new information requirements, we again awaken every bill collector, provide the necessary information for it to change its programatic (as opposed to genetic) codes, and allow it to return to sleep. Just as in the global data collection case, we can perform this sort of change during off hours, and there is rarely a case where we need such a change on a moment's notice. We needn't use this sort of systemic evolution all of the time. Instead, we can take the less invasive approach of developing better and better bill collectors over time, and simply birthing them for collecting new bills. Eventually older bill collectors die out as they conclude their tasks.

Our first viral bill collector was implemented by one programmer in one week, in 1986. It has evolved successfully in response to new needs without any global changes since that time, and although this sort of evolution requires human design, the amount of work is minimal. The bill collection viruses also coexist in the environment with a set of 'maintenance' viruses that periodically awaken to perform cleanup tasks associated with systems maintenance.

Maintenance Viruses and the Birth/Death Process

Maintenance viruses, as a class, seem to be one of the most useful forms of computer viruses in existence today. Put in the simplest terms, computer systems are imperfect, and these imperfections often leave residual side effects, such as undeleted temporary files, programs that never stop processing, and incorrectly set protection bits. As more and more of these things happen over time, systems become less and less usable, until finally, a human being repairs the problems in order to continue efficient processing.

In the case of the viral bill collector, the design of the system is such that temporary files are stored under identifiable names, processing times for each bill collector tends to be relatively short, and protection bits are consistently set to known values. To reduce manual systems administration, we decided to implement viruses that replicate themselves in limited numbers, seek out known imperfections, and repair them. Over time, we reduced systems administration to the point where the viral bill collector operated for over two years without any systems administration other than adding and removing users. The maintenance viruses were so successful that they even removed side effects of other failed maintenance viruses.

To assure the continued survival of the maintenance viruses, they are born with a particular probability every time a user awakens a bill collector, and to assure they don't dominate processing by unbounded growth, they have limited life spans and replicate with lower probability in each successive generation. With proper probabilities, this combination of factors successfully produces stable populations of maintenance viruses and is quite resilient.

Another interesting way to control population ratios is with the technique described earlier for defeating vaccination. By simply having a partitioned code space used to indicate which viruses can replicate, you can control population ratios quite resiliently with no centralized control. You get birth with a probability related to the available food, while death of each strain is guaranteed by the life of other strains.

These "birth/death" processes are central to the problem of designing viruses that don't run amok, as well as to the evolution of viral systems over time. If it weren't for the death of old bill collectors and maintenance viruses, the system would eternally be collecting bills and performing maintenance under old designs, and the number of bill collectors and maintenance viruses would grow without bound. A global modification of all of the existing bill collectors would be required to make a system change, and this might be very hard to accomplish in a complex network. Birth and death processes appear to be vital to optimization in viral systems where the environment changes dramatically with time, since what is optimal today may not even survive tomorrow.

Toward Random Variation and Selective Survival

We have spoken of evolution, but to many, this concept doesn't seem to apply to computer programs in the same way it applies to biological systems. In its simplest form, we speak of systems evolving through human reprogramming, and indeed, the term evolution seems to accurately describe the process of change a system goes through in its life cycle, but this is only one way that programs can evolve.

Consider a bill collector that uses pseudo-random variables to slowly change the weighting of different collection strategies from generation to generation, and replicates individual bill collectors with a probability associated with their profitability (the net fee collected after all expenses of collection). In this case, assuming that the parameters being varied relate to the success of the collection process in an appropriate manner, the 'species' of available viruses for the collection process will seem to 'evolve' toward a more profitable set of bill collectors.

If we use less variation on bill collectors that are more successful, we may tend toward local optima. To attain global optima, we may occasionally require enough randomness to shake loose from local optima. Over time, we may find many local optima, each with a fairly stable local population of bill collectors. Thus different species of bill collectors may coexist in the environment if there are adequate local niches for their survival. Cross breeding of species is feasible by taking selected parameters from different species to birth new bill collectors. Some will thrive, while some will not even survive. As the external environment changes, different species may perform better, and the balance of life will ebb and shift. This evolutionary process is commonly called "random variation and selective survival", and is roughly the equivalent of biological evolution as we now commonly speak of it.

More Complex Behavior

The behavior we are discussing is getting complex, involving local and global optimization, evolution over time, and even the coexistence of species in an environment; and yet the computer programs we are discussing are still quite simple. Our viral bill collectors consist of only a few pages of program code, and yet they perform the same tasks carried out by much larger programs. The inclusion of evolution in experimental systems has been accomplished in only a few lines of program code. We create a small "generating set" of instructions which creates a complex system over time through birth/death processes, random variation and selective survival, and the interaction of coexisting species in the environment. Even quite simple generating sets can result in very complex systems. In fact, in many cases, we cannot even predict the general form of the resulting system.

Our inability to accurately predict systemic behavior in complex systems stems, in general, from the fact that it is impossible to derive a solution to the halting problem. More specifically, it was proven that a virus can evolve in as general a fashion as a computer can compute, and therefore that the result of viral evolution is potentially as complex as Turing's computation. It seems there is little we can do about predicting the behavior of general purpose evolutionary systems, but just as there are large classes of computer programs with predictable behavior, there are large classes of evolutionary systems with predictable behavior.

In the same way as we can generate computer programs from specifications, we can generate evolutionary systems from specifications, and assure to a reasonable degree that they will act within predefined boundaries. In the case of the maintenance virus, we can even get enhanced system reliability with viral techniques. Unfortunately, we haven't yet developed our mathematical understanding of viruses in an environment to the point where we can make good predictive models of these sorts of systems, but there is a general belief that many important problems are not intractable at the systemic level, and if that is true, we may be able to make good predictive models of the behavior of large classes of useful viral systems.

One of the ways we can design predictable viral systems is by adding communications. Completely deaf and dumb viruses have a hard time surviving because they tend to be born and die without any controlling influences, and we get unstable situations which either consume too many resources and ruin the ecology or die from lack of sufficient biomass. With even rudimentary communications, viruses seem to survive far better. For example, most real-world computer viruses survive far better if they only infect programs that are not yet infected. The competing viruses in the environment discussed earlier use a rudimentary form of communications to differentiate food. Too much communication also makes viruses inefficient, because they have to address an increasingly global amount of information. We suspect that communication is beneficial to viral survival at a rudimentary level only to the extent that it helps to form stable population relative to the resources in the environment, but in terms of designing predictable viral systems, communications seems to be key.

The maintenance viruses described earlier provide a good example of viral communication. There is no 'direct' communication between the maintenance viruses, but they end up communicating in the sense that what each virus does to the environment alters the actions of other viruses. For example, a maintenance virus that deletes temporary files that haven't been accessed in 24 hours or more will not delete any files that a previous maintenance virus has already deleted, since the earlier virus already consumed them. Since the latter virus acts differently based on the actions of the earlier virus, there is a rudimentary form of communication between the viruses via changes in the environment. In fact, humans communicate in much the same way; by making changes in the environment (e.g. sound waves) that affect other humans.

The Computer Virus Contest

The possibilities for practical viruses are unbounded, but they are only starting to be explored. Unfortunately, viruses have gotten a bad name, partly because there are so many malicious and unauthorized viruses operating in the world. If the computing community doesn't act to counter these intrusions soon, society may restrict research in this area and delay or destroy any chance we have at exploiting the benefits of this new technology. There are now many useful tools for defending against malicious viruses and other integrity corruptions in computer systems, and they can often be implemented without undue restriction to normal user activity, but perhaps another tactic would also serve society well.

The tactic is simple; instead of writing malicious viruses, damaging other people's computer systems, hiding their identity, and risking arrest, prosecution, and punishment; virus writers could be provided with a legitimate venue for expressing their intellectual interest, and get both positive recognition and financial rewards for their efforts. By changing the system of rewards and punishment, we may dramatically improve the global virus situation and simultaneously harness the creative efforts of virus writers for useful applications.

One instance of such a tactic is the 'Computer Virus Contest' run by ASP Press, which gives an annual cash prize for the most useful computer virus submitted. The contest rules prohibit the use of viruses that have been released into uncontrolled environments, viruses placed in systems without explicit permission of the owner, and viruses without practical mechanisms to control their spread. For further information on the Computer Virus Contest, use the enclosed Order Form to request information.

A S P

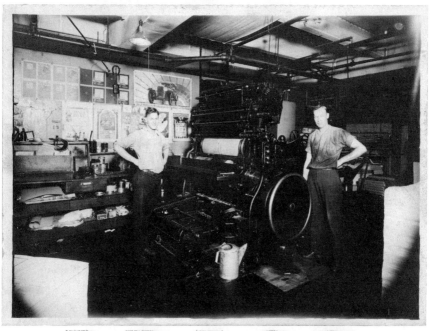

PRESS